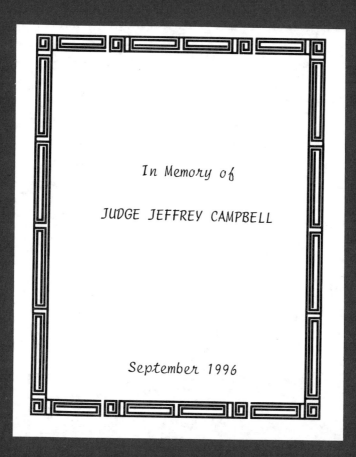

In Memory of

JUDGE JEFFREY CAMPBELL

September 1996

O-KEE-PA

Plate I.   Mandan Woman, Chief, and Warrior

O-KEE-PA

A RELIGIOUS CEREMONY

AND OTHER

CUSTOMS OF THE MANDANS

BY

GEORGE CATLIN

EDITED AND WITH AN INTRODUCTION BY

JOHN C. EWERS

WITH THIRTEEN COLORED ILLUSTRATIONS

UNIVERSITY OF NEBRASKA PRESS

LINCOLN AND LONDON

Library of Congress Cataloging in Publication Data

Catlin, George, 1796–1872.
    O-kee-pa, a religious ceremony, and other customs
of the Mandans.

    Reprint of the ed. published by Yale University
Press, New Haven.
    Bibliography: p.
    Includes index.
    1. O-kee-pa (Religious ceremony) 2. Mandan In-
dians. I. Ewers, John Canfield. II. Title.
[E99.M2C3   1976]   299'.7   76–4522
ISBN 0–8032–5845–3

Bison Book edition published in 1976 by arrangement with Yale University Press.

PREFACE TO THE
CENTENNIAL EDITION

The idea of preparing a Centennial Edition of George Catlin's *O-kee-pa* had its inception in a conversation I had with my friend, Archibald Hanna, Jr., William Robertson Coe Curator of Western Americana, Yale University Library, while we were attending the annual meeting of the Western Historical Association in Helena, Montana, in the fall of 1965. I agreed to edit the new edition and to write an introduction which would tell the modern reader how the famous American painter, George Catlin, came to write this once controversial book, and estimate its importance to American Indian studies. Meanwhile Mr. Hanna, with characteristic effectiveness, laid our plan before the Publications Committee of the Yale University Press.

This new edition faithfully reproduces the now rare first edition of Catlin's *O-kee-pa*, first published concurrently by Trübner and Co., of London, and Lippincott of Philadelphia, in 1867. The colored illustrations and page size are the same, and the type is similar to that of the first edition. It has been found necessary to correct only a few spellings and to delete some excessive quotation marks in the original text. Catlin's Appendix has been preserved, and his *Folium Reservatum*, which accompanied only the few copies of the first edition that were delivered to scholars, is included. Besides my introduction, footnotes, and index, the only other addition is the testimony of the fur trader James Kipp, who witnessed the O-kee-pa in George Catlin's company: *On the Accuracy of Catlin's Account of the Mandan Ceremonies;* this was first published by the Smithsonian Institution soon after Catlin's death in 1872.

I am grateful to Anne Wilde for her editorial assistance. And I am most appreciative of the care Yale University Press has taken in reproducing this century-old classic in American ethnology.

JOHN C. EWERS

Smithsonian Institution
Washington, D.C.
January 1967

CONTENTS

LIST OF PLATES

INTRODUCTION

AN APPRECIATION OF GEORGE CATLIN'S *O-KEE-PA*

No other Indians of the American West held such a fascination for early explorers and fur traders as did the Mandans of the Upper Missouri in the years before they were decimated by a tragic plague of smallpox in 1837. And no other white man did so much to interpret primitive Mandan life and culture to the civilized world as did that pioneer American artist and amateur ethnologist of the Upper Missouri—George Catlin. Five summers before that destructive smallpox epidemic, Catlin visited the Mandans in their picturesque earth-lodge villages near the trading post of Fort Clark, at the mouth of the Knife River in present North Dakota. He painted numerous portraits of their prominent chiefs and womenfolk and pictured their village life, their amusements, dances, religious ceremonies, and burial ground. In his exceedingly popular two-volume work, *Letters and Notes on the Manners, Customs and Condition of the North American Indians,* published at his own expense in London in 1841, Catlin vividly described and extravagantly praised the Mandans as the most remarkable of the more than forty Indian tribes he had met in his wide travels beyond the frontiers of white settlement. Yet none of his voluminous writings and numerous paintings was so severely and unjustly criticized in his own time as were his frank descriptions and revealing pictures of the major Mandan religious ceremony—the O-kee-pa—which he witnessed in midsummer 1832 in the open plaza and in the large ceremonial lodge fronting on that plaza in the center of a Mandan village.

THE MANDANS BEFORE GEORGE CATLIN'S VISIT

In order to fully appreciate George Catlin's contributions to an understanding of the Mandans and their religious life we must view them in the context of what is known of the Mandans from other sources. In recent years archaeologists have studied intensively the Indian sites on the Missouri River in the Dakotas, many of which have already been lost to future study by the construction of large dams and the filling of extensive reservoirs along the Missouri main stream. Archaeologists now inform us that they have found indications of plazas and adjoining ceremonial lodges (i.e. structures of larger size than the normal dwellings) in the remains of small prehistoric villages in the Missouri Valley between the mouth of the White River in South Dakota and that of the Little Missouri in North Dakota. These village sites date back to the years between 1100 and 1400 of the Christian era. Before about 1400 these ceremonial complexes were on the periphery of unfortified villages. But in more recent prehistoric villages they were located in the centers of larger, more compact, fortified towns with estimated populations of nearly a thousand Indians. This evidence from the ground seems to suggest that the O-kee-pa was performed some four hundred to seven hundred years before George Catlin witnessed and first described this unique Indian ceremony in 1832, and that it became increasingly important as a cohesive force in Mandan Indian society in subsequent years. However, the archaeological record can tell us nothing of the use of distinctive costumes, body paints, and ceremonial paraphernalia, or of the detailed nature of the rituals in this elaborate primitive ceremony.[1]

1. The evidence from these prehistoric sites is presented in W. Raymond Wood, *An Interpretation of Mandan Culture History*. Bureau of American Ethnology (in press).

Nearly a century before Catlin visited the Mandans, the first white man was attracted to their Missouri River villages. Pierre Gaultier de Varennes de la Verendrye, a French fur trader and avid seeker of a water route across North America to the Western Sea, first learned from nomadic Assiniboine and Cree Indians, who hunted buffalo on the plains west of the Red River of the North, of a strange people who lived in large villages on a great river far to the southwest. His Indian informants told him they obtained corn in trade with those people. They led La Verendrye to believe that the strangers were a tall, bearded, fair-skinned people who built substantial forts and houses like the French. That was in 1734.

Four years later, in October 1738, La Verendrye accompanied an Assiniboine trading party overland from Fort La Reine, on the Assiniboine River near present Portage la Prairie, west of Winnipeg, Manitoba. Near the mouth of the Heart River on the Missouri he found the strangers living in six large villages. He marveled at their skill in constructing sizable earth-covered houses, the cleanliness of their streets, and the stoutness of the fortifications that surrounded their settlements. He observed that these people were shrewd traders who consistently bested the Assiniboine in their exchange of corn, tobacco, skins, and colored plumes, for the European-made guns, axes, kettles, powder, bullets, knives, and awls which the Assiniboine middlemen had obtained from white men's posts in their own country. La Verendrye observed that these strangers—the Mandans —dressed like the Assiniboines, "being naked except for a garment of buffalo skin carelessly worn without any breechclout." But after a stay of only eight days in their villages he concluded: "This tribe is of mixed blood, black and white. The women are rather handsome, particularly the light-colored ones; they have an abundance of fair hair."[2]

Thus the first white visitor to the Mandans found them in 1738 already operating a flourishing native trading center on the Upper

2. *Journal and Letters of Pierre Gaultier de Varennes de la Verendrye*, ed. Lawrence J. Burpee, Toronto, 1927, pp. 154, 305-54.

Missouri, and already in possession of some useful metal weapons and utensils of white men's manufacture. But he made no observations on the complex and prolonged religious ceremonies of the Mandans during his brief residence in their villages.

Decades passed; Great Britain replaced France in the north, and Spain acquired the vast territory of Louisiana in 1763. But the Mandans continued to play their role as the master traders of the Upper Missouri. A few Frenchmen established themselves in the Mandan villages, took Indian wives, learned the Mandan language, and served as guides and interpreters for occasional small parties of British traders who journeyed overland to the Mandans from their trading posts farther north.

Meanwhile, rumors spread among white men of a tribe of Welsh-speaking Indians living in a remote area of the American West. An obscure Welsh legend affirmed that Madoc, the son of a prince of North Wales, had embarked on an overseas expedition in the year 1170 and had never returned. It was easy for imaginative Welshmen to believe that Madoc had discovered America and that Welsh-speaking Indians, descendants of members of his party, must still be found somewhere in the vast American wilderness.

Perhaps Jacques D'Eglise, the first trader from St. Louis to explore the Missouri as far as the Mandan villages in 1790, added some fuel to this fire when he reported that the Mandans "are white like Europeans, and much more civilized than any other Indians."[3]

In 1793 a young man arrived in St. Louis on a curious mission. He was John Thomas Evans, son of a Welsh minister, who had been encouraged by a group of Welshmen in London to come to America to search for Welsh-speaking Indians. He reached St. Louis at a fortunate time. On October 15, 1793, a group of St. Louis merchants founded the Company of Explorers of the Upper Missouri, with exclusive rights to trade with the Indians in the area of their explorations. Evans obtained employment with this company and in 1795

---

3. Trudeau to Carondolet, St. Louis, Oct. 20, 1792, in *Before Lewis and Clark; Documents Illustrating the History of the Missouri, 1785–1804*, ed. A. P. Nasatir, *1*, 161.

made his first journey up the Missouri. Hostile Sioux prevented him from reaching the Mandans that year, but in 1796 he was more successful, spending more than six months—from late September to the spring of 1797—among the Mandans. He returned to civilization with a discouraging report for Dr. Samuel Jones of Philadelphia, a proponent of the Madoc theory. "In respect of the Welsh Indians, I have only to inform you that I could not meet with such a people, and from the intercourse I have had with the Indians from latitude 35 to 49, I think you may with safety inform our friends that they have no existence."[4]

The St. Louis traders failed to follow up their trade contacts with the Mandans in the years immediately after John Evans' disillusioning quest. The French agents of British traders remained entrenched in Mandan villages. Early in the winter of 1797 one of them, René Jussome, guided David Thompson of the North West Company and nine free traders overland from Macdonald's House on the Assiniboine to the Mandan villages. Thompson was disgusted with the lack of chastity of the Mandan women, which his white comrades found "almost their sole motive for their journey hereto; the goods they brought, they sold at 50 to 60 pr cent above their cost; and reserving enough to pay their debts, and buy some corn; spent the rest on Women." During the twelve days he spent among the Mandans (December 30, 1797, to January 10, 1798), Thompson was told of a summer ceremony of three days' duration, on the last day of which Mandan women gave themselves to men other than their husbands, and he noted laconically, "The Mandans have many ceremonies, in all of which the women bear a part, but my interpreter treated them with contempt; which perhaps they merited."[5]

David Thompson also reported that some sixteen years earlier the Mandan population had been greatly reduced by an epidemic of

4. John Evans' quest for Welsh-speaking Indians on the Upper Missouri is well described within the framework of the interests in the Madoc theory at the time in David Williams, "John Evans' Strange Journey"; the quotation is from p. 526 of No. 3.

5. *David Thompson's Narrative of his Explorations in Western America, 1784–1812*, p. 234.

smallpox. They now occupied but two villages and a portion of a third, with an average population of about ten to a lodge. He estimated their total number at only 1,520, 220 of whom were warriors. Yet he noted that through intensive cultivation of their alluvial bottomlands, with only rude hoes and digging sticks for gardening implements, these Indians raised enough corn, pumpkins, and small beans to feed themselves and to trade to their nomadic Indian neighbors.[6]

Only seven years later Captains Lewis and Clark, leading their Corps of Discovery up the Missouri on their epic overland trek to the Pacific Ocean, met the Mandans in two villages below the mouth of the Knife River and estimated their total population at only 1,250. Lewis and Clark spent the winter of 1804–05 near the Mandans in a rude fort which they named Fort Mandan in their honor. These friendly Indians supplied the exploring party with corn and furnished much valuable information on the resources of their region and on the Indian tribes and the country the travelers would see on their way westward the following spring. Lewis and Clark also came to know the importance of buffalo meat to the Mandan diet and of buffalo products in the material culture of these Indians. They experienced the difficulties of finding buffalo near the Mandan villages during the cold months, and described an elaborate Mandan winter ceremony for calling the buffalo, in which some of the members of their party participated:

> 5th Jany. 1805, Buff[alo]e Dance—a dance for the benefit of the old men. They, about the time Buffe. is scarce, appoint a man to harangue village saying buffe. is far off & they must have a feast to bring them back—name a certain night & place for it. The young married men prepare provisions (a platter) pipe & tobacco which they take to the feast—their wives accompy. them with nothing on except a robe or mantle round them—

6. Ibid., pp. 227–31.

feast in a house—the old men assemble first seat thems[elves] in a ring on skins cross legged around a fire in the middle of the house. They have before them a sort of small doll dressed like a woman—when the young men & their [wives] arrive the young man chooses the old one whom he means to favor—& to whom he gives the provisions—the old men eat—after which the young man gives the old man a lighted pipe & smokes with him—the [young man] then asks the old man in a whining tone to do him honor in indulging himself with his wife which he brings up to him—the old man follows the woman out of the door. After smoking a particular o.m. appointed for the purpose takes the image in his arms carries her out of doors lies down on it with the appearance of copulation. This is the signal for the young men who are in the rear of the circle with their wives behind them to lead them up to o.m. naked except for the robe. The woman arrived out of doors unfolds her robe lies down & invites & receives his embraces. Sometimes the o.m. can scarcely walk. If the old man wants to get a present from husband goes only to the door—the wife informs the husband who sends for a robe & some articles of dress & throws at the feet of the old man & begs that he will not despise or disgrace him, but return to his wife. If present insufficient still lingers till increased by husband. If he receives it he is bound to go. The o.m. if he cannot do the substantial service must go thro' the forms which saves the honor of the parties. This ceremony over—the o.m. smoke together & the y.m. dance together. Indian women do not dance together ever. White men are always considered as o.m. & are generally preferred by the Squaws because they will give probably some present and for other obvious reasons.[7]

7. This description of the Mandan buffalo-calling ceremony, from the notes of Nicholas Biddle, first editor of Lewis and Clark's narrative of their travels, was first published in *English* in *Letters of the Lewis and Clark Expedition with Related Documents, 1783–1854*, ed. Donald Jackson, p. 538.

In this first detailed description of a complex Mandan religious ceremony we find an account of deliberate sexual activity outside the bonds of wedlock which tended to brand primitive Mandan women as unchaste in the opinion of civilized whites. Whether the early explorers and traders were fascinated or disgusted by what they saw or heard of this activity in the Mandan villages, it seems certain that they did not understand it. The religious life of the primitive Mandan was dominated by a continuous search for "power"—an intangible sacred element—whose proof of existence could be observed only in the effects attributable to it by the believer in it—the avoidance of ill health and misfortune and the attainment of success and a long life.

In the religious context of the buffalo ceremony which Lewis and Clark described, the wives of active young men offered themselves to their ceremonial fathers, old and/or distinguished men who were thought to possess much "power." Through intimate relations with them, women obtained this power so that they might in turn pass it on to their husbands. The success of this transmission could be judged only by whether it achieved the desired results—in this case bringing herds of buffalo near enough to the village so that the husbands could kill them and bring in meat for their hungry families.

Likewise, this Mandan concept of the transmission of power through sexual intercourse seemed to have played a part in the eagerness of Mandan women to cohabit with white men in the early days of the fur trade. Even though a present was expected, its value was of little consequence to the Indian woman in comparison with the opportunity to acquire power from her white lover. And Lewis and Clark observed that "the Indians believed that these traders were the most powerful persons in the nation."[8]

Alexander Henry, a North West Company trader, spent all of

---

8. *History of the Expedition under the command of Lewis and Clark,* ed. Elliott Coues, *4,* 1217.

ten days among the Mandan in the latter part of July 1806. He observed:

> They seem to be a very lascivious set of people. The men make no scruple in offering their wives to strangers without solicitation, and are offended if their favors are not accepted, unless convinced that there is some good reason for your refusal, and that it is not out of contempt. They expect payment for their complaisance, but a mere trifle will satisfy them—even one single coat button.[9]

As Edward M. Bruner has recently observed, "It does not seem reasonable that a shrewd trading people such as the Mandan would be satisfied with a coat button."[10] Surely a less tangible but more valuable commodity was involved in such transactions in the minds of Mandan husbands and wives—the transfer of the white man's "power."

Henry described the plazas in the Mandan villages: "About the center of each village is an open space of about four acres, around which the huts are regularly built at equal distances, fronting the open space."[11] And it seems just possible that he reached the Mandans late in the last day of the O-kee-pa, on July 19, 1806, for he noted:

> About midnight we were awakened by some extraordinary noise in the village. On going to the outer door I saw about 25 persons of both sexes, entirely naked, going about the village singing and dancing. At times they withdrew in couples, but soon rejoined their companions in the dance and song. During this short separation from the rest they appeared to be very closely engaged, and notwithstanding the night was dark I could perceive them occupied in enjoying each other with as little

9. *New Light on the Early History of the Greater Northwest*, ed. Elliott Coues, *1*, 342.
10. Edward M. Bruner, "Mandan," in *Perspectives in American Indian Culture Change*, p. 217.
11. *New Light on the Early History of the Greater Northwest*, p. 338.

ceremony as if it had been only the common calls of nature. This affair continued about two hours, during which they made the tour of the village several times. What was the meaning of this ceremony I could not learn; but certainly there could be no performance more lascivious than the one I witnessed.[12]

American fur traders from St. Louis gained control of the Mandan trade during the next decade. But it was a full quarter of a century after Alexander Henry that George Catlin visited the Mandan and provided the next and most substantial contribution to our understanding of Mandan ceremonialism. It is important to recognize, however, that during this interval James Kipp, as a fur trader among the Mandans, gained their confidence and a working knowledge of their language. As early as 1823 Kipp established a fort near the Mandans for the Columbia Fur Company. In 1831 he built the American Fur Company's post, Fort Clark, within easy walking distance of the two Mandan villages. He was in charge of that post during the summer of 1832 when George Catlin arrived. And without Kipp's assistance in introducing him to the Mandans it seems improbable that Catlin could have established a rapport with these primitive people that would have enabled him to witness the entire performance of their O-kee-pa that summer.

GEORGE CATLIN AMONG THE MANDANS

Catlin was younger in energy and enthusiasm than in years that summer of 1832. Actually he passed his thirty-sixth birthday while he was studying the Mandans. He had been born in Wilkes-Barre, Pennsylvania, July 26, 1796. As a mere boy his interest in American Indians was aroused by Indian legends and stories of Indian captivity which were told in his neighborhood. His own mother, as a girl, had been taken prisoner by Indians during the bloody Wyoming Valley massacre of 1778. And he bore on his cheek the mark of a tomahawk

12. Ibid., p. 327. Henry may have witnessed the ritual which Catlin described as "Feast of the Buffaloes," a sequel to the performance of the O-kee-pa. See pp. 69–71 of this volume.

that had glanced off a tree and hit him in the face while he was play-
ing Indian with other boys. Catlin spent much of his youth outdoors,
hunting, fishing, and collecting flint arrowheads and other Indian
relics. And he grew strong and wiry—but never very tall.

Although he had been more interested in nature than in school-
books, Catlin's lawyer father induced him to enter the law school of
Reeves and Gould at Litchfield, Connecticut, in 1817. The next
year he passed his bar examinations and began the practice of law
in Lucerne, Pennsylvania. But his heart was not in the courtroom;
he was becoming more and more interested in art. Finally he sold
his law books, abandoned his legal career, and moved to Philadelphia to devote full time to painting.

As a painter Catlin was entirely self-taught. With characteristic
energy he worked at his art until he developed skill as both minia-
turist and portrait painter in oils. In 1824 he was elected an academi-
cian of the Pennsylvania Academy of Fine Arts, a select group that
included such masters of the period as Charles Willson Peale, Rem-
brandt Peale, and Thomas Sully. In 1828, twelve of Catlin's works
were exhibited by the American Academy of Fine Arts. One of these
was a full-length portrait of the late Governor De Witt Clinton of
New York State, which Catlin painted for the Corporation of the
City of New York.

The fame of his sitters and the acceptance of his paintings in important exhibitions indicated that Catlin was achieving success as a
portraitist of fine ladies and gentlemen. But he was restless and dis-
satisfied. He was, as he later wrote, "continually reaching for some
branch or enterprise of the arts on which to devote a whole life-time
of enthusiasm."[13]

While he was seeking to find himself, Catlin saw some ten or
fifteen Indian members of a delegation from the wilds of the "Far
West," who were passing through Philadelphia on their way to visit
their Great White Father in Washington. The sight of their hand-

---

13. George Catlin, *Letters and Notes on the Manners, Customs and Condition of the
North American Indians,* vol. 1, p. 2.

some features and picturesque costumes rekindled Catlin's boyhood enthusiam for Indians; it changed the course of his career and provided him with a goal for his life's work. In later years he worded his new resolve thus:

> Man in the simplicity and loftiness of his nature, unrestrained and unfettered by the disguises of art, is surely the most beautiful model for the painter, and the country from which he hails is unquestionably the best study or school of the arts in the world; such I am sure, from the models I have seen, is the wilderness of North America. And the history and customs of such a people, preserved by pictorial illustrations are themes worthy of the life-time of one man, and nothing short of the loss of my life, shall prevent me from visiting their country, and of becoming their historian.[14]

Catlin's first experience in painting Indians was gained among the acculturated and peaceful Iroquois—reservation Indians of western New York. His earliest known Indian portrait was an unfinished likeness of the noted Seneca orator, Red Jacket, signed and dated "Buffalo, 1826."

Yet Catlin early recognized that the greatest opportunities for recording Indians on canvas were to be found among those tribes who lived far beyond the frontiers of white settlement, who still preserved their traditional cultures. And he realized that he had better hurry to capture these Indians with his pencil and paintbrush before they too were depopulated by wars and disease and their age-old customs lost as the frontier of settlement marched westward.

Catlin began his great western adventure in St. Louis in the spring of 1830. There he won the friendship of William Clark, co-leader of the famed Lewis and Clark expedition, who was then Superintendent of Indian Affairs for the western tribes. With the help of Clark and his various Indian agents in the field, Catlin gained the opportunity to meet and to paint a number of the tribes living

14. Ibid.

on the Great Plains south of the River Platte during 1830 and 1831, including the Pawnee, Omaha, Iowa, Missouri, Kanza, and Sauk and Fox.

Then, in April 1832, after two years of western experience, Catlin seized the unique opportunity of traveling two thousand miles up from St. Louis aboard the American Fur Company's *Yellowstone,* the first steamboat to travel upriver as far as Fort Union, the Company's finest post, at the mouth of the Yellowstone. It was on this trip that Catlin began to paint western landscapes and scenes from Indian life, as well as Indian portraits, and to submit letters containing his fresh field observations to the *New-York Commercial Advertiser.*

On its way up the Missouri, the steamboat stopped at Fort Pierre, the Company's post at the mouth of the Teton for trade with the warlike western Sioux, and Catlin availed himself of the opportunity to picture Indian life in the vicinity of that establishment. At Fort Clark he gained his first view of the Mandans, and it must have been enough to convince him that he should spend some time among them on his return downriver. The *Yellowstone* reached Fort Union on June 16, 1832, and Catlin spent a month there painting magnificently dressed Assiniboine, Blackfoot, Crow, Cree, and Plains Ojibwa visitors to that post, hunting buffalo on horseback, and picturing the buffalo hunt and other typical activities of the nomadic tribes.

Then shortly after mid-July Catlin set out in a small skiff, with two French-Canadian trappers for company, down the muddy Missouri. They must have left Fort Union about July 16 and reached Fort Clark about July 22, for Catlin wrote that the journey required seven days, and his letter dated "August 5th, 1832, Mandan Village, Upper Missouri", stated that he had resided at this place for "about two weeks."[15]

---

15. Ibid., vol. 1, p. 79. Catlin's letter of August 5, 1832, was published in the *New-York Commercial Advertiser,* Nov. 13, 1832. However, a later letter on the Mandans, dated "Mandan Village, August 20, 1832," could not have been written at that place, for the Fort

Catlin observed that the Mandans then numbered 1,600 to 1,800 persons. He found:

> nothing in their personal appearance or demeanor to distin-
> guish them in any considerable degree from the neighboring
> Indians, excepting the singular appearance of their hair. . . .
> Their hair has all the shades and variety of colours that are to be
> seen amongst white society. Many children, male and female, at
> the age of 10 or 15 years, are seen with their hair of a bright
> silvery grey, and some almost perfectly white.[16]

Catlin managed to persuade two of the Mandan chiefs to pose for him. This was a completely new experience for the Mandans, whose own picture-writing rendered men in the form of crude stick-like figures. As Catlin's likenesses of the chiefs developed on his canvas, the villagers crowded around him. Only a few days thereafter, he wrote:

> The eager curiosity and expression of astonishment with
> which they gazed upon me, plainly showed that they considered
> me some strange being. They soon resolved that I was the
> greatest *medicine* man in the world, for they said I had made
> living beings—they said they could see them laugh, and if
> they could laugh they could speak, &c. and must be alive. The
> squaws soon raised a cry against me in the village, saying that
> I was a dangerous man, that if I could make living persons by
> looking at them, I could kill them when I pleased, and that
> some bad luck would happen to those whom I painted. In this
> way they excited fears in the minds of a number of Chiefs who
> had agreed to sit; my operations were, of course, completely at
> a stand. I finally had an interview with a number of them, and

Pierre *Journal* for August 14, 1832, recorded that "Messrs. Catlin and Bogart arrived from Fort Union on their way to St. Louis," and Fort Pierre was nearly 350 miles downstream from the Mandan villages. See the extracts from the Fort Tecumseh and Pierre *Journal*, in H. M. Chittenden, *The American Fur Trade of the Far West, 3,* 981.

16. *New-York Commercial Advertiser,* Nov. 13, 1832.

assured them that I was but a man like themselves—that my
art had no *medicine* or mystery about it, but could be learned
by any of them if they would practise it as long as I had—that
my intentions towards them were of the most friendly kind—
and that in the country where I lived, *brave* men never allowed
their squaws to frighten them with their foolish whims, stories,
&c: they all arose, shook me by the hand, and dressed themselves
for their pictures. There was no difficulty after that about sit-
tings, all were ready to sit—the squaws were silent—and my
painting room a continued resort for them, where they waited
with impatience to see the completion of each picture, that
they could laugh, sing a new song, &c. &c. I was then often taken
by the arm by the Chiefs and led to their lodge, where a treat
was prepared for me in their best style. In this manner I was
taken from one lodge to another, and treated in the most
cordial manner.[17]

So it was that this first white artist to picture the primitive
Mandans gained acceptance among them as *medicine white man.*
And Catlin, roused to a feverish pitch of creativity, took advantage
of his opportunity to execute at least twenty portraits and as many
scenes in Indian life during his stay of at most three weeks in the
vicinity of Fort Clark.

Probably it was Catlin's newly won status as a medicine man
as well as James Kipp's persuasion that won the traveling artist
permission to witness the annual religious ceremony of the Mandans, the O-kee-pa, which must have been performed near the
middle of Catlin's stay at Fort Clark. Writing his first published
description of this ceremony on August 12, 1832, shortly after he
had seen it and both his notes and his memory were fresh, Catlin
claimed that he had witnessed "every form and feature of these rites"
of four days' duration, including "the whole preparation of their
secret medicines and *hocus pocus* operations, together with the hor-

17. Ibid.

rible scenes of cruelty which they practised upon their own bodies."
And he had followed the performances with such fascination that
"most of the time [I was] too much engaged to think of my meals."[18]
He closed this brief description with the statement:

> I have made four paintings which will embrace the whole
> of these scenes, and I intend to publish them to the world with
> the certificates of the two gentlemen who were with me, *that I
> have nothing extenuated nor aught set down in malice.*[19]

Nine years later Catlin explained: "I took my sketchbook with
me, and have made many and faithful drawings of what we saw, and
full notes of everything as translated to me by the interpreter."
And he claimed that the "four paintings of these strange scenes,
containing several hundred figures, representing the transactions of
each day" were painted in the Mandan village "in an earth-covered
wigwam, with a fine sky-light over my head."[20]

These paintings, hurriedly rendered in the enthusiasm of the
moment, became part of Catlin's famed Indian Gallery and were
exhibited with it in the towns of the Ohio Valley and prominent
cities of the East in the 1830s, as well as in London and Paris in the
1840s. They are now preserved in the University Museum, University
of Pennsylvania, in Philadelphia.[21]

CATLIN'S PUBLISHED ACCOUNTS OF THE O-KEE-PA

During the next thirty-five years Catlin published not one but
three descriptions of the Mandan O-kee-pa. The first was a con-
densed account, penned on August 12, 1832, while the experience
of seeing the performance was very fresh in his mind. It appeared

---

18. *New-York Commercial Advertiser,* Jan. 10, 1833.
19. Ibid.
20. George Catlin, *Letters and Notes, 1,* 155.
21. These are Cat. Nos. 38429 through 38432 in the collections of the University Museum.
The paintings were listed and briefly described as Nos. 491 through 494 in the earliest known
exhibition *Catalogue of Catlin's Indian Gallery,* New York, 1837.

as a four-column article in the *New-York Commercial Advertiser* for January 10, 1833, over George Catlin's signature.

The second account was not published until nine years after Catlin had witnessed the ceremony. Meanwhile Catlin had traveled widely in the Indian country of the western Great Lakes, the upper Mississippi Valley, and on the southern plains in present Oklahoma, painting Indians of more than a score of tribes and filling his notebooks with his firsthand observations as well as information about Indians obtained in conversations with knowledgeable frontiersmen —traders, Indian agents, army officers, and others. In 1836 he saw and painted the famous quarry near present Pipestone, Minnesota, where Indians obtained and traded widely the red pipestone which was named "catlinite" in the artist's honor two years later.[22]

As his paintings grew in number, Catlin embarked upon a second career of exhibiting his works to the public. From a modest opening in Pittsburgh in 1833, he progressed to a successful New York showing in 1837, followed by exhibitions in other large eastern cities. Catlin's fondest hope was that the Congress of the United States would purchase his entire collection, including his more than five hundred paintings and the numerous artifacts he had obtained from various sources over a period of years. Such an action would reward him for his efforts, keep his memory green, and afford Americans of his own and future generations a unique opportunity to learn about the native peoples of their own country.

Disappointed in his first of many efforts to sell his collection to the United States, Catlin packed his paintings and artifacts and live grizzly bears and sailed for England aboard the steam packet *Roscius* on November 25, 1839. He could not have foreseen that thirty-two years would pass before he would see New York again. The following February first he opened his exhibition in Egyptian Hall in London. And twenty months later Catlin published his first and most impor-

---

22. Dr. Charles Thomas Jackson, mineralogist, of Boston, analyzed this Indian pipestone, found it to be a new compound, and named it "catlinite" (*The American Journal of Science and Arts, 35,* 1838–39, p. 388).

tant Indian book, *Letters and Notes on the Manners, Customs and Condition of the North American Indians,* profusely illustrated with small steel engravings, most of them copied from his oil paintings. The book was well received by reviewers and became exceedingly popular in the United States and abroad. Fully a quarter of this two-volume work was devoted to Catlin's favorite tribe—the Mandans. One chapter was devoted to an expanded description of the O-kee-pa, with four illustrations of the ceremony in progress. Catlin described the excruciating self-torture, to which some of the men who participated in the ceremony submitted themselves, in vivid and gruesome detail. But he avoided a frank description of the sexual symbols and activities connected with the performance. He suggested these mysterious rites—and perhaps gave undue emphasis to them—by inserting successions of pseudo-Indian words in place of the true details. In Victorian England in the year 1841 writers did not describe fertility rites in books written for popular distribution.

In 1845 Catlin received the highest honor any artist of his time could imagine—a private showing of his works in the world-famous Louvre in Paris, attended by the French King Louis Philippe. This event marked the summit of his career as an exhibitor. Yet Catlin's exhibitions abroad had never been money-making enterprises over any extended periods. By mid-century he was in dire straits. In 1852 his entire collection was about to be sold at auction to pay his debts when Joseph Harrison, a very successful locomotive designer and builder from Philadelphia, paid off most of Catlin's obligations and took the collection back to America to place it in dead storage.

While traveling in South America in a vain attempt to recoup his fortunes, Catlin received an alarming letter from his friend Baron Alexander von Humboldt, the noted German naturalist. Written from Potsdam and dated June 9, 1856, it read in part:

An immense scrap-book on the North American Indians, written by Schoolcraft for the Government of the United States, in three huge volumes, has been sent to me as a present, and I find, in looking into it, that he denies the truth of your descriptions of the "Mandan religious ceremonies," distinctly saying that they are contrary to the facts, and that they are the works of your imagination, &c.

Now, my dear and esteemed friend, this charge, made by such a man as Schoolcraft, and "under the authority of the Government of the United States," to stand in the libraries of the scientific institutions of the whole civilized world, to which they are being sent as presents from your Government, is calculated not only to injure your hard-earned good name, but to destroy the value of your precious works through all ages, unless you take immediate steps with the Government of your country to counteract its effects.

I have often conversed with our illustrious traveler in America, the Prince Maximilian, of Neuwied, who spent a winter with the Mandans subsequent to your visit to them, and gained information from the chiefs entirely corroborating your descriptions. You should write to the prince at once, and, getting a letter from him (with your proofs) lay it before the Government of your country, which cannot fail, by some legislative act, to do you justice.[23]

Catlin recalled that the pompous Henry Rowe Schoolcraft had come to London in 1846 to induce him to contribute illustrations for a voluminous work on the Indians of the United States which he was planning, and he had turned Schoolcraft down because he preferred to publish his own pictures. With funds appropriated by Congress, Schoolcraft had proceeded to collect data on the Indians from various sources and to compile an expensive, six-volume work bearing the impressive title, *Historical and Statistical Information Respecting the History, Condition and Prospects of the Indian Tribes of the United States,* which was published at government

---

23. George Catlin published this letter in his book, *The Lifted and Subsided Rocks of North America,* p. 221.

expense in Philadelphia during the years 1851–57. To the third
volume of that work David D. Mitchell, then Superintendent of
Indian Affairs in St. Louis, who had been active in the Indian trade
of the Upper Missouri during 1830–40, contributed a two-page
article on the Mandan Indians. His concluding sentences read: "Information as to their peculiar customs can be found in the Journal
of Lewis and Clark. The scenes described by Catlin, existed almost
entirely in the fertile imagination of that gentleman."[24] In the fifth
and sixth volumes, Schoolcraft himself, who had never seen the
Mandans, took Catlin to task both for his enthusiastic espousal of
the Madoc theory of Mandan origin and his claim that the Mandans
were extinct, in Catlin's 1841 book.[25]

It was the cruel statement by Colonel Mitchell that irritated
Catlin, for it implied that he had not described truthfully what he
had seen with his own eyes in a Mandan village during the summer
of 1832. Catlin also believed that as long as this blot remained on
his good name he would have little hope of selling his collection in
his own country or abroad. The criticism was to plague Catlin for
the rest of his life, and it helped to make this proud, self-centered
artist a rather bitter old man. But Mitchell died in 1861, and Schoolcraft in 1864, before Catlin launched what he believed would be
the effective counterattack Baron von Humboldt had outlined to
him. And then he was galvanized into action by another severe blow
to his ego.

There appeared in London in the year 1865 a sixty-seven-page
pamphlet bearing the half-title *An Account of an Annual Religious
Ceremony Practised by the Mandan Tribe of North American
Indians by George Catlin.* This pamphlet was described in *Trübner's American and Oriental Literary Record,* No. 6 (August 21,
1865) as an interesting little monograph, of which only fifty copies
had been privately printed and distributed to a very select circle,

24. Henry Rowe Schoolcraft, compiler, *Historical and Statistical Information Respecting
the History, Condition and Prospects of the Indian Tribes of the United States, 3,* 254.
25. Ibid., vol. 5, pp. 59–60; vol. 6, p. 486.

since the character of the work would not bear wide circulation. There can be little doubt that George Catlin was the author of this unexpurgated description of the O-kee-pa. It may have been printed from the manuscript of a lecture he had delivered to the Philobiblon Society of London in response to an invitation to tell in plain English what he had seen of the ceremony in 1832. When he learned of this shameful exploitation of his confidences, Catlin wrote a strong letter which was published in the next number of *Trübner's American and Oriental Literary Record*, September 21, 1865, in which he called this privately printed pamphlet "a gross and mangled extract from my account of the Mandan religious ceremony printed and circulated without my permission or knowledge; of which I have demanded the surrender of every copy printed; and for any reprint or circulation of the same I will prosecute."[26]

That Trübner and Co. managed to make their peace with Catlin seems to be proven by the fact that they were the publishers of Catlin's third and last published description of the ceremony— *O-KEE-PA: A Religious Ceremony; and other Customs of the Mandans*—in 1867.

In preparing this book (here reproduced in its entirety on the centennial of its first publication) Catlin followed Baron von Humboldt's suggestions, carefully collecting his "proofs" and appending them to his description of the ceremony. Apparently he felt obliged to counter Schoolcraft's criticisms of his adherence to the Madoc theory of Mandan origin and also his statement that the Mandan were extinct, for he devoted a section of "Remarks" to a statement of his "proofs" of Welsh origin of the Mandan, and included two letters he had received from the Upper Missouri after the smallpox epidemic of 1837, which appeared to prove that the Mandan no longer

26. This unauthorized publication of Catlin's description of the O-kee-pa is now a rarity. In an article, *"A Rare Pamphlet on the Mandan Religious Ceremony, in the Library of the Horniman Museum,"* L. J. P. Gaskin stated that he had been able to trace only two other copies of this pamphlet—one in the New York Public Library, the other in the Henry Huntington Library, California. However, there is a fine copy in the Western Americana Collection, Yale University.

existed. And to further substantiate the high regard which respected Americans held for his works, Catlin added statements by Lewis Cass and Daniel Webster in praise of his accomplishments.

Catlin did not neglect to follow Baron von Humboldt's advice in seeking a testimonial from the aged Prince Maximilian also, for he knew that this able German scientist had wintered among the Mandans a year after his own visit to them and had obtained from James Kipp and Indian informants sufficient information to prepare his own description of the ceremony for his scholarly work, *Reise in das innere Nord-America in den Jahren 1832 bis 1834,* which had been translated and published in English in London (1843) while Catlin was in that city.

Bruxelles, December 2, 1866.

Dear Prince,

Since we travelled together on the upper Missouri, Mr. Schoolcraft, who has published a large work on the North American Indians for the United States Government, and who never had the industry or the courage to go within 1000 miles of the Mandans, has endeavoured to impeach my descriptions of the Mandan religious ceremonies, which, as the tribe has become extinct, he has supposed rested upon my testimony alone. In his great work under the authority of the government, and presented to the literary and scientific Institutions of the whole civilized world, he has denied that those voluntary tortures ever took place, and has attributed them to my "very fertile imagination" tending therefore, to deprive Ethnology of the most extraordinary custom of the North American Indians, and to render my name infamous in all future ages, unless I can satisfactorily refute so foul a calumny.

Your Highness spent the winter with the Mandans, subsequent to the summer season in which I witnessed those ceremonies, and of course lived in the constant society of Mr. Kipp, the Fur trader at that post, who witnessed in company with me the whole of those four days ceremonies, and interpreted every thing for me, and from whom you no doubt drew a detailed account of those scenes as we saw them, together.

I send you with this letter my four oil paintings of those 4 days ceremonies, made as they now are, in the Mandan village, and seen and approved by the chiefs and the whole tribe, and having attached to their backs the certificates of Mr. Kipp and two other men who were with us, that these paintings represent strictly what we saw, and without exaggeration.

I send you also herewith, the manuscript of a work (O-kee-pa) descriptive of those ceremonies, which I am about to publish; and on reading this and examining my paintings, you will be able to inform me and the world, how far my descriptions of these scenes will be supported by information gathered by yourself, from Mr. Kipp and others during the winter which you spent in the Mandan village, and for which I shall feel deeply indebted.

Your Highness'
Obedient servant
Geo. Catlin[27]

Eighteen days later the 84-year-old Prince Maximilian sent his gracious reply from his Rhineland castle in Neuwied, Prussia. And Catlin proudly printed his letter opposite his own preface to this new book as a testimonial to the accuracy of his own observations.

Recognizing the value to scientists of a more frank description of a portion of the ceremony than he deemed proper to include in his account for the general reader, Catlin also published a *Folium Reser-*

---

27. Both Catlin's letter to Maximilian and the Prince's letter of reply were printed on facing pages by Trübner of London, the publishers of Catlin's *O-kee-pa*, presumably as an advertisement for Catlin's book. We are grateful to the New York Public Library for permission to reprint George Catlin's letter of December 2, 1866, from the copy in the Rare Book Room of that library.

vatum for the information of serious scholars who study "not the *proprieties* of man, but *Man*." The insert is included in this new edition (pp. 83–85) in order to provide Catlin's complete description of the Mandan ceremony which he witnessed in 1832.[28]

Catlin planned to travel from Brussels to Washington in the fall of 1868 to present an appeal to Congress asking that copies of his *O-kee-pa* be purchased by the United States government and sent to each of the libraries and other repositories in the world to which Schoolcraft's defamatory books had been sent—and thus to clear his good name. But the times were not propitious, and Catlin remained in Brussels completing a new series of Indian paintings on cardboard—much-reduced and combined figures from his earlier oil paintings—which he termed his "Cartoon Collection." Not until the fall of 1871 did Catlin return to New York to exhibit his cartoons. In February 1872, at the invitation of Joseph Henry, Secretary of the Smithsonian Institution, Catlin hung what was to be the last exhibition of his own works in a large gallery of the Smithsonian building in Washington. Henry also provided the artist with living quarters in one of the third-floor tower rooms of the building, and assisted Catlin with his petition to Congress. But by fall Catlin became ill, and when Henry's physician pronounced his condition as "Bright's disease—an incurable illness"—Catlin was moved to the home of his brother-in-law in Jersey City, where he died on December 23, 1872, at the age of 76 years.[29]

28. The proof and revised proof of this three-page statement are in the Western Americana Collection, Yale University. The former, dated May 11, bears the title "(Discretion)," which Catlin crossed out, and the author's handwritten corrections, as well as his statement, "I think the above should be printed on a tinted paper. G.C.," at the bottom of the last page. The *Folium Reservatum* here reprinted [on pp. 83–85] follows the revised proof of May 17 (1867).

29. The exhibition of Catlin's "cartoons" at the Smithsonian Institution in 1872, and the great concern of Joseph Henry for the artist's health and comfort during his last illness, are recorded in Joseph Henry's Diary for the period February 19, 1872, through December of that year, and in his correspondence during those months in the Archives of the Smithsonian Institution.

Plate II. Bird's-eye View of the Mandan Village

Plate III.   Interior of the Medicine Lodge

History's Verdict of Catlin's *O-kee-pa*

Joseph Henry, brilliant physicist and first Secretary of the Smithsonian Institution, was the first American scientist of stature to stoutly defend George Catlin's integrity as a field observer. As "an act of justice to the memory of the late Mr. Catlin" he published in the *Annual Report of the Board of Regents of the Smithsonian Institution* within a few months of Catlin's death a statement "On the Accuracy of Catlin's Account of the Mandan Ceremonies," by the 85-year-old retired fur trader, James Kipp, who had witnessed the O-kee-pa with Catlin and had interpreted for him while the artist was in the Mandan villages in 1832. This strong endorsement of the artist's account was written just four months before George Catlin's death. It is reprinted here on pages 93–94.

But the wise Joseph Henry knew that scientific truth was not something that could be determined by acts of Congress. As early as March 16, 1866, he had written to Catlin's daughter, Elizabeth,

> I have no hesitation in saying that your father's valuable collections of Indian portraits ought to be purchased by the General Government and carefully preserved as a monument of the race which our encroachments upon their territory have consigned to premature extinction; and more than that an appropriation should be made for at least assistance in the publication of the great work on the North American Indians which your father has for so many years been engaged in elaborating.[30]

Yet on April 1, 1870, after he had read Catlin's memorial to Congress beseeching that august body to distribute copies of his *O-kee-pa* to libraries and learned societies throughout the world in order to counteract the harm done to his reputation by Schoolcraft, Henry

---

30. Joseph Henry to Miss E. W. Catlin, March 16, 1866; Smithsonian Institution Archives.

wrote Catlin: "Truth, however, is mighty and will prevail, whether Congress intervenes in the matter or not."[31]

When we look back upon this historic controversy in American anthropology from the vantage point of the passage of a century, it is easier to assess the truth than it was in Henry's day.

Obviously, Catlin was severely handicapped by the fact that he was never able to revisit the Upper Missouri tribes after the destructive smallpox epidemic of 1837, and that he was for thirty-two years after 1839 in virtual exile from his own country—completely out of touch with the traders, government officials, and scholars who knew the Mandan Indians during that period. For Schoolcraft was right that Catlin was misinformed regarding the extinction of the Mandans in 1837. They suffered terrible losses. They were more than literally decimated by that epidemic, yet of the estimated 1,800 Mandans prior to the plague, 123 or more (including at least 23 men) survived. The remnant united with the survivors of the other farming tribes of the Upper Missouri, the Hidatsa and Arikara, and by 1862 occupied the one village of Like-a-Fishhook, on the Missouri River, adjoininig the trading post of Fort Berthold. There they continued to perform their sacred O-kee-pa until 1889 or 1890.[32]

In 1858 Henry A. Boller, a young Philadelphian who admired Catlin's writings and paintings, entered the fur trade as a clerk at Fort Atkinson, near Like-a-Fishhook. Late in July of that year he witnessed the "Religious Ceremony" of the Mandans, and wrote his brother on August 18, 1858:

> I assure you that Catlin has truthfully painted and described it. I have seen the "bulls" dancing round the "big tub" in the center of the Village, the young men fasting in the Medicine

31. Joseph Henry to George Catlin, April 1, 1870; Smithsonian Institution Archives.

32. In 1930 Alfred W. Bowers' aged Mandan informants told him that the O-kee-pa rites were slightly altered and simplified after the smallpox epidemic of 1837, but the ceremony was performed until prohibited by an army officer in charge of Fort Berthold Reservation about 1890. Bowers, *Mandan Social and Ceremonial Organization*, pp. 105, 119, 150.

Lodge, and also the fearful hanging to poles; the last days pro-
ceedings I did not see, owing to a pelting rain.[33]

At Fort Berthold two summers later (August 20–22, 1860), Lieu-
tenant Henry E. Maynadier witnessed and described in detail "a
peculiar ceremony of the Mandans." His account of it, published
in the *Report of Brevet Brigadier General W. F. Raynolds on the
Exploration of the Yellowstone and the Country Drained by That
River* as a Senate Executive Document in 1868, is of unique interest
in the history of O-kee-pa studies. Maynadier believed these rites
had "never before been described," and so he could not have been
influenced by Catlin's writings and pictures. His description also
appears to be the last detailed account of the O-kee-pa to have been
written by an eyewitness:

> I had made a present of my epaulettes to the chief Four Bears,
> and in this way had obtained the run of the village and access
> to the most sacred places.
>
> In the centre of the village is a circular space some 150 feet
> in diameter, with commodious scaffolds ranged around it, which
> answer the double purpose of seats for the spectators and places
> to dry corn and squashes. In the centre of the open space is a
> circular enclosure of slabs 10 or 12 feet high, and about 4 feet
> in diameter. This is called the "big canoe," and has a very
> decided reference to the flood, as the tradition which I will
> relate further will show. The first day of the ceremony the
> proceedings were commenced by five men, ranging themselves
> in front of the big canoe, with drums made of skins, shaped like
> turtles, and said to be filled with water. I believe, though, that
> they were stuffed with hair, with a hoop to keep them distended
> and make them give out when struck a sound like a drum.
> After these were arranged, a man, stripped to the skin and

33. "The Letters of Henry A. Boller: Upper Missouri Fur Trader," p. 162. In his book,
Among the Indians: Eight Years in the Far West, pp. 100–11, Boller described the O-kee-pa
as the "great Bull Medicine" of the Mandans, a four-day ceremony, which included the
torture feature.

smeared with white clay, came from the Medicine lodge opposite the big canoe, and, walking behind the canoe, leaned
against it and hid his face in his hands. At the same time a
woman, in a short skirt, with her legs scarred and bleeding,
her hair cut short, and several bleeding wounds in her forehead
and breasts, leaned against the side of the canoe and began
crying and howling most piteously, the drummers all the time
thumping away and chanting in unison. This woman was the
relative of a young man who had been killed a short time pre-
viously by the Rees. Having sung his praise and exhibited her
grief by her scarifications, she went away, and some 10 or 15
objects bounded into the arena. These were men painted in a
grotesque manner, wearing buffalo heads with strips of fur down
their backs and long branches of willow fastened to their arms.
The drummers beat and howled, the buffalo men danced and
capered in admirable precision, and waved their willow branches like wings, everybody shouted, dogs barked, and the motions
of the dancers became more and more violent. Two of the
buffalo men would run together and butt with their heads,
and, indeed, they imitated all the motions of a herd of buffalo.
Suddenly the drummers rose, snatched up their drums and ran
into the Medicine lodge, followed by the individual who had
been leaning against the canoe, the buffalo disappearing among
the lodges. Then came an old man who dug a hole in the ground
about 20 feet in front of the canoe and erected a stout post 15
feet high, having two cords fastened at the top and looped at the
ends. The drummers came out of the Medicine lodge, took their
places, and the young man who, in the first performance had
stood behind the canoe was led to the foot of the post by the
two villainous-looking old medicine men.

This young man had been three days without meat or drink,
and being perfectly naked and smeared with clay he looked
ghastly. Kneeling on the ground, one of the old men took up
a portion of the skin of the young man's breast and passed a

knife through it, making two apertures with a strip of skin between. The blood trickled down, and the victim winced perceptibly. A skewer of wood four inches long was passed through the two holes, and the loop at the end of one of the cords placed over its two ends. The second cord was fastened in like manner to the other breast, and the poor wretch lifted to his feet. The drummers thumped, and the young man threw himself violently back, bearing his whole weight on the cords, and swinging round the foot of the pole. The skin drew out several inches, and seemed to stretch further at every jerk of the poor fellow, who pulled, and tossed, and especially when, after four or five minutes, nature claimed her sway, and the poor wretch fainted and hung collapsed. He was not touched, and, seeming to revive, renewed his efforts to bring the tortures to a close by breaking the ligaments of skin which held the skewers. After half an hour or more the skin broke and he was carried off.

The next victim was served even more dreadfully, though he bore it remarkably well. The skewers were passed under the skin of the back, just above the shoulder blades, and he was hung up to a scaffold with his feet three feet from the ground. Then more skewers were inserted in the fleshy parts of the arms and legs, and buffalo skulls hung to them. I was amazed to see how far the skin would stretch, pulling out a distance of 12 or 15 inches.

These disgusting scenes were repeated during two days, varied by races round the big canoe by troops of young men and boys, dragging from four to ten buffalo heads attached to skewers in their backs. Some fainted and did not recover; some were violently nauseated, and proved conclusively that their three days' fast had not been faithfully kept; others held out to the end, and leaped, kicked, and struggled until they were free from their disagreeable attachments.

All the implements, skewers, bull heads, cords, and willow branches were deposited inside the big canoe, and were considered sacred from that time out. I endeavored to ascertain what all this meant, but could only get a meagre account. The idea of the big canoe is common among several tribes, and others infer that it is based upon some tradition of the deluge. The Mandans relate a story agreeing in many respects with our account of the flood. They say that their fathers came to this country in a large canoe, and after having been many days on the water a bird flew out to them, bearing a willow branch with fresh leaves on it. They soon after landed and drew the canoe on land to live in. The bird remained with them, and showed them how to build earthen lodges, and where to find game and fruit. This bird is even now held sacred, and enters largely into their religious symbols. The self-torture and mutilation which accompanied their mysteries cannot be explained, except by the supposition that it is a course of preparation for the hardships and dangers of war. I noticed that every male over 10 years old had the scars of the skewer holes on his breast and back.[34]

It was unfortunate that Mitchell and Schoolcraft did not live to read this vivid corroboration of Catlin's descriptions of the self-torture in the Mandan O-kee-pa, written by an officer of the United States Army on the basis of what he saw with his own eyes. It is ironic that George Catlin had not learned of the publication of this very detailed description *in a Senate document two years before* he petitioned Congress to protect his reputation by distributing copies of his *O-kee-pa* to the libraries of the world.

Two years later Lewis Henry Morgan, now recognized by many anthropologists as the "father of American anthropology," was engaged in ethnological fieldwork among the tribes of the Upper Missouri. He arrived at Fort Berthold on June 27, 1862, the day

---

34. Brevet Brig. Gen. W. F. Raynolds, *Report on the Exploration of the Yellowstone,* pp. 149–51. Presumably Maynadier had no knowledge of Catlin's description of the O-kee-pa when he witnessed the ceremony in 1860, but mention of Catlin in the published report indicates that he must have read the artist's 1841 book before he wrote his account of his field experiences for publication.

after a four-day annual religious ceremony had been concluded, but he obtained a brief account of it from a young man who had witnessed it that year as well as in former years. Morgan must have been mistaken in calling this a Minnetare (Hidatsa) ceremony, for his brief description clearly indicates that it was the Mandan O-kee-pa, in which, at that time, a number of Hidatsa Indians may also have participated. Not only does Morgan's account describe the self-torture, but it corroborates some of the description in Catlin's *Folium Reservatum:*

> There was one person who personated either a clown or the Evil Spirit. He wore a mask, was painted black, with white rings, and red spots in the middle. On his back was painted the new moon. He wore a beaver skin bonnet, and showed in front the male organ in wood of large size, with buffalo hair pendant. All in the ring yielded him precedence.[35]

This character was undoubtedly Catlin's O-ke-hée-de (the owl or Evil Spirit) portrayed in Plate IV of this volume.

Dr. Washington Matthews, army physician and pioneer field ethnologist, had a fine opportunity to study the Indians of Like-a-Fishhook Village during the years 1869–72 while he was stationed at nearby Fort Buford. He observed that the central plaza, medicine lodge, and ark were still parts of that settlement, and "Within the temple and around the ark, the Mandans still perform the ceremony of the Okeepa, which Catlin so accurately describes."[36]

Other students of the Mandans have sought to dissociate Catlin's objective descriptions of what he saw among the Mandans from his

35. *Lewis Henry Morgan, The Indian Journals,* pp. 193–95. Compare p. 83 of Catlin's description in this volume. Morgan also mentioned the impersonation of buffaloes, bears, antelopes, and snakes in this ceremony by about forty costumed performers. He briefly described the self-torture and suggested that the "government ought to prohibit these cruel usages."

36. Washington Matthews, *Ethnography and Philology of the Hidatsa Indians,* p. 10. Matthews added: "The awful severities of the rite have, however, been somewhat mitigated since his [Catlin's] day."

romantic enchantment with the old theory of the Welsh origin of
that tribe. Ferdinand V. Hayden, noted scientific explorer of the
Upper Missouri during the 1850s, whose interest in Indians was
scarcely less marked than his love for geology, thought Catlin's descriptions of Mandan customs were "highly colored" but "for the
most part, correct. The notion which he entertained that the Mandans are of Welsh origin has become so thoroughly exploded, that
it is unnecessary to allude to it further."[37]

The anthropologists George F. Will and Herbert J. Spinden, co-
authors of the first scholarly monograph on the Mandans, published
by the Peabody Museum of Archaeology and Ethnology of Harvard
University in 1906, see no reason to fault Catlin's field observations
because of his untenable theories:

> Catlin became a great supporter of the wild theory that the
> Mandans were of Welsh origin; little of this appears, however,
> in his main work, and his facts have not interfered with his
> theories. His drawings are probably a little idealized, but they
> too, afford a reasonably accurate source of information.[38]

They paid a high tribute to George Catlin by not attempting to
describe the Mandan O-kee-pa, concluding: "No description is
necessary as Catlin has given two very full ones and Maximilian has
also given a good account of it."[39]

In the most recent volume on the Mandans, devoted primarily
to a study of their religion and ceremonies, Alfred W. Bowers leans
heavily upon the recollections of aged members of the tribe whom
he interviewed during the 1930s. They were the last generation of
Mandans to have seen an O-kee-pa ceremony. Yet it is apparent that
Bowers was guided by Catlin's and Prince Maximilian's accounts of
the O-kee-pa in questioning his Indian informants, and he illustrates

---

37. F. V. Hayden, "Contributions to the Ethnography and Philology of the Indian Tribes
of the Missouri Valley," p. 434.
38. G. F. Will and H. J. Spinden, "The Mandans. A Study of Their Culture," p. 87.
39. Ibid., p. 143.

his chapter on that ceremony with reproductions of Catlin's pictures, first published in *O-kee-pa* a century ago.[40]

With the passage of time Catlin's *O-kee-pa* has ripened into a nineteenth-century classic in the ethnology of western North America. It was the first account of a complex Plains Indian religious ceremony to be both written and illustrated by an eyewitness to that ceremony. It was the first account of the major ceremony of the tribe that possessed the richest ceremonial development of any tribe of the Upper Missouri—the Mandans. Surely it is not perfect. But if we do not permit George Catlin's untenable theories of Mandan origin to interfere with our appreciation of his narration of the O-kee-pa, we should find that it is still a lively and a more than reasonably accurate account of a unique, primitive American religious drama.

40. Alfred W. Bowers, *Mandan Social and Ceremonial Organization;* Chapter 4 of this volume (pp. 111–63) is devoted to "The Okipa Ceremony."

O-KEE-PA

A RELIGIOUS CEREMONY

AND OTHER

CUSTOMS OF THE MANDANS

LETTER FROM PRINCE MAXIMILIAN OF NEUWIED

"Neuwied, Prussia, December 20, 1866.

To Mr. George Catlin.

Dear Sir,

Your letter came safely to hand, and revived the quite forgotten recollections of my stay amongst the Indian tribes of the Missouri, now thirty-three years past.

The Mandan tribe, which we both have known so well, and with whom I passed a whole winter, was one of the first to be destroyed by a terrible disease, when all the distinguished chiefs, Mah-to-toh-pa, Char-a-ta, Numa-ka-kie, etc. etc., died; and it is doubtful if a single man of them remained to record the history, customs, and religious ideas of his people.

Not having been, like yourself, an eye-witness of those remarkable starvations and tortures of the *O-kee-pa,* but having arrived later, and spent the whole of the winter with the Mandans, I received from all the distinguished chiefs, and from Mr. Kipp (at that time director of Fort Clarke, at the Mandan village, and an excellent interpreter of the Mandan language), the most detailed and complete record and description of the *O-kee-pa* festival, where the young men suffered a great deal; and I can attest your relation of it to be a correct one, after all that I heard and observed myself.

In my description of my voyage in North America (English edition) I gave a very detailed description of the *O-kee-pa,* as it was reported to me by all the chiefs and Mr. Kipp, and it is about the same that you told,—and nobody would doubt our veracity, I hope.

I know most of the American works published on the American Indians, and I possess many of them; but it would be a labour too heavy for my age of eighty-five years, to recapitulate them all.

Schoolcraft is a writer who knows well the Indians of his own part of the country, but I do not know his last large work on that matter. If he should doubt what we have both told in our works, of the great Medicine festivities of the *O-kee-pa,* he would be wrong, certainly.

If my statement, as that of a witness, could be of use to you, I should be very pleased.

Your obedient
(Signed)   Max, *Prince of Neuwied."*

PREFACE

All men have, or ought to have, some peculiar ambition towards the attainment of which the principal energies of their lives are directed: mine, which developed itself some thirty years since, has been that of perpetuating the looks and customs of a numerous race of human beings fast passing to extinction. In this pursuit I have passed fourteen years of my life amongst the various tribes of Indians in North, South, and Central America, and of the numerous customs which I have recorded, there is nothing else so peculiar and surprising as the O-kee-pa of the Mandans, the subject of this book,—an annual ceremony, which I described in a former publication, but which description, forming but an item in a large work, was necessarily too brief to give all the connecting links of a custom which derives its interest from being understood in all its phases.

This publication, therefore, which is made for all classes of readers, as well as for gentlemen of science who study, not the *proprieties* of man, but *Man,* and which has not before appeared in all its parts, is made from a sense of *duty,* to perpetuate entire a human custom of extraordinary interest, peculiar to a single tribe in America, and which tribe, as will be seen, is now extinct; leaving in my hands alone chiefly, what has been preserved of their personal looks and peculiar modes.

GEO. CATLIN.

O-KEE-PA

A RELIGIOUS CEREMONY OF THE MANDANS

In a narrative of fourteen years' travels and residence amongst the native tribes of North and South America, entitled *'Life amongst the Indians,'* and published in London and in Paris, several years since, I gave an account of the tribe of Mandans,—their personal appearance, character, and habits; and briefly alluded to the singular and unique custom which is now to be described, and was then omitted, as was alleged, for want of sufficient space for its insertion, —the "O-kee-pa," an annual religious ceremony, to the strict observance of which those ignorant and superstitious people attributed not only their enjoyment in life, but their very existence; for traditions, their only history, instructed them in the belief that the singular forms of this ceremony produced the buffaloes for their supply of food, and that the omission of this annual ceremony, with its sacrifices made to the waters, would bring upon them a repetition of the calamity which their traditions say once befell them, destroying the whole human race, excepting one man, who landed from his canoe on a high mountain in the West.[1]

This tradition, however, was not peculiar to the Mandan tribe, for amongst one hundred and twenty different tribes that I have visited in North and South and Central America, not a tribe exists that has not related to me distinct or vague traditions of such a calamity, in which one, or three, or eight persons were saved above the waters, on the top of a high mountain. Some of these, at the base of the Rocky Mountains and in the plains of Venezuela, and the Pampa del Sacramento in South America, make annual pilgrimages to the fancied summits where the antediluvian species were saved in canoes or otherwise, and, under the mysterious regulations of their *medicine* (mystery) men, tender their prayers and sacrifices to the Great Spirit, to ensure their exemption from a similar catastrophe.

Indian traditions are generally conflicting, and soon run into fable; but how strong a proof is the *unanimous* tradition of the aboriginal races of a whole continent, of such an event!—how strong a corroboration of the Mosaic account,—and what an unanswerable proof that *anthropos Americanus* is an antediluvian race! And how just a claim does it lay, with the various modes and forms which these poor people practise in celebrating that event, to the inquiries and sympathies of the philanthropic and Christian (as well as to the scientific) world!

Some of those writers who have endeavoured to trace the aborigines of America to an Asiatic or Egyptian origin, have advanced these traditions as evidence in support of their theories, which are, as yet, but unconfirmed hypotheses; and as there is not yet known to exist (as I shall show, but not in this place), either in the American languages, or in the Mexican or Aztec, or other monuments of these people, one single proof of such an immigration (though it could have been made), these traditions as yet are mine, and not theirs,— are American,—indigenous, and not exotic. If it were shown that inspired history of the Deluge and of the Creation restricted those events to one continent alone, then it might be that the American races came from the Eastern continent, bringing these traditions with them; but until that is proved, the American traditions of the Deluge are no evidence whatever of an Eastern origin. If it were so,

Plate IV.   The Bull-Dance

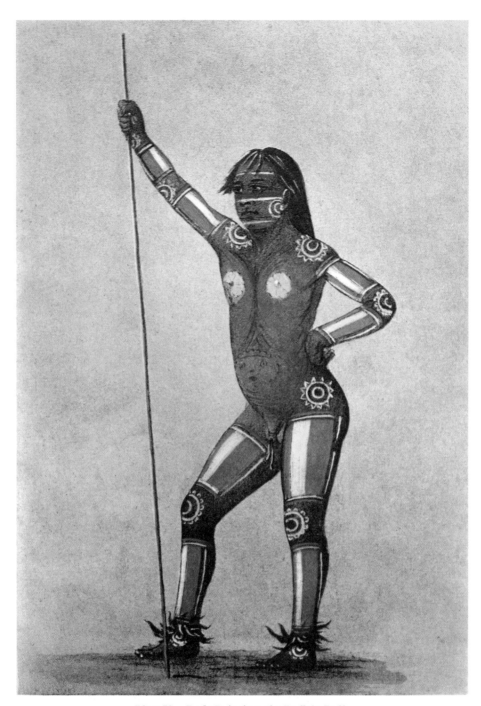

Plate V.   Body Painting of a Buffalo Bull

Plate VI. A Buffalo Bull Dancing

Plate VII.   Dancers Symbolizing Night and Day

and the aborigines of America brought their traditions of the Deluge from the East, why did they not bring inspired history of the *Creation?*[2]

Though there is not a tribe in America but what have some theory of man's creation, there is not one amongst them all that bears the slightest resemblance to the Mosaic account. How strange is this if these people came from the country where inspiration was prior to all history! The Mandans believed they were created under the ground, and that a portion of their people reside there yet. The Choctaws assert that "they were created *craw-fish,* living alternately under the ground and above it, as they chose; and coming out at their little holes in the earth to get the warmth of the sun one sunny day, a portion of the tribe was driven away and could not return; they built the Choctaw village, and the remainder of the tribe are still living under the ground."

The Sioux relate with great minuteness their traditions of the creation. They say that "the Indians were all made from the red pipe-stone, which is exactly of their colour; that the Great Spirit, at a subsequent period, called all the tribes together at the red pipe-stone quarry, and told them this, that the red stone was their flesh, and that they must use it for their pipes only."

Other tribes were created under the water; and at least one half of the tribes in America represent that man was first created under the ground, or in the rocky caverns of the mountains. Why this diversity of theories of the *Creation,* if these people brought their tradition of the Deluge from the land of inspiration?

This interesting subject, too intricate for full discussion in this work, will be further incidentally alluded to in the course of the following relations.

For the scientific, who look amongst these native people chiefly for shapes of their skulls and for analogies to foreign races, I believe there will be found enough in the following description of their religious ceremonies to command their attention; and for the purely philanthropic and religious world, whose motives are love and sympathy, there will be sufficient to excite their profoundest astonishment, and to touch their hearts with pity.

In a relation so singular, and apparently incredible, as I am now to make, I hope the reader will be able to follow me, under the conviction that I am representing nothing in my descriptions or in my illustrations but what I *saw,* and that I had by my side, during the four days of these scenes, three civilized and educated men, who gave me their certificates that they witnessed with me all these scenes as I have represented them, and which certificates, with other evidences, will be produced in their proper places, as I proceed.

During the summer of 1832 I made two visits to the tribe of Mandan Indians, all living in one village of earth-covered wigwams, on the west bank of the Missouri river, eighteen hundred miles above the town of St. Louis.[3]

Their numbers at that time were between two and three thousand, and they were living entirely according to their native modes, having had no other civilized people residing amongst them or in their vicinity, that we know of, than the few individuals conducting the Missouri Fur Company's business with them, and living in a trading-house by the side of them.

Two exploring parties had long before visited the Mandans, but without in any way affecting their manners. The first of these, in 1738, under the lead of the Brothers Verendrye, Frenchmen, who afterwards ascended the Missouri and Saskachewan, to the Rocky Mountains; and the other, under Lewis and Clark, about sixty years afterwards.[4]

The Mandans, in their personal appearance, as well as in their modes, had many peculiarities different from the other tribes around them. In stature they were about the ordinary size; they were comfortably, and in many instances very beautifully clad with dresses of skins. Both women and men wore leggings and moccasins made of skins, and neatly embroidered with dyed porcupine quills. Every man had his "tunique and manteau" of skins, which he wore or not as the temperature prompted; and every woman wore a dress of deer or antelope skins, covering the arms to the elbows, and the person from the throat nearly to the feet.

In complexion, colour of hair, and eyes, they generally bore a family resemblance to the rest of the American tribes, but there were exceptions, constituting perhaps one-fifth or one-sixth part of the tribe, whose complexions were nearly white, with hair of a silvery-grey from childhood to old age, their eyes light blue, their faces oval, devoid of the salient angles so strongly characterizing all the other American tribes, and owing, unquestionably, to the infusion of some foreign stock.[5]

Amongst the men, practised by a considerable portion of them, was a mode peculiar to the tribe, and exceedingly curious,—that of cultivating the hair to fall, spreading over their backs, to their haunches, and oftentimes as low as the calves of their legs; divided into flattened masses of an inch or more in breadth, and filled at intervals of two or three inches with hardened glue and red or yellow ochre.[6]

I here present (Plate I.) three of my Mandan portraits in their ordinary costume,—a chief, a warrior, and a young woman,—lest the reader should form a wrong opinion of their usual appearance, from the *bizarre* effects of the figures disguised with clay and other pigments in the ceremony to be described in this work.

The Mandans (*Nu-mah-ká-kee*, pheasants, as they called themselves) have been known from the time of the first visits made to them to the day of their destruction, as one of the most friendly and hospitable tribes on the United States frontier; and it had become a proverb in those regions, and much to their credit, as they claimed, "that no Mandan ever killed a white man."

I was received with great kindness by their chiefs and by the people, and afforded every facility for making my portraits and other designs and notes on their customs; and from Mr. J. Kipp, the conductor of the Fur Company's affairs at that post, and his interpreter, I was enabled to obtain the most complete interpretation of chiefly all that I witnessed.

I had heard, long before I reached their village, of their "annual religious ceremony," which the Mandans call *"O-kee-pa,"* and from Mr. Kipp, who had resided several years with the people, a partial account of it; and from him the most pressing advice to remain until the ceremony commenced, as he believed it would be a subject of great interest to me.

I resolved to await its approach, and in the meantime, while inquiring of one of the chiefs whose portrait I was painting, when this ceremony was to begin, he replied that "it would commence as soon as the willow-leaves were full grown under the bank of the river." I asked him why the willow had anything to do with it, when he again replied, "The twig which the bird brought into the *Big Canoe* was a willow-bough, and had full-grown leaves on it."[7]

It will here be for the reader to appreciate the surprise with which I met such a remark from the lips of a wild man in the heart of an Indian country, and eighteen hundred miles from the nearest civilization; and the eagerness with which I followed up my inquiries on a subject so unexpected and so full of interest.

I inquired of him what bird he alluded to, which he found difficulty in making me understand, and, taking me by the arm, he conducted me through the winding avenues of the village until he discovered a couple of mourning doves pecking in the side of one of the earth-covered wigwams, and pointing to them said, "There is the bird; it is great *medicine*." It then occurred to me that on my arrival in their village Mr. Kipp had cautioned me against harming these birds, which were numerous in the village, and guarded and protected with a superstitious veneration as great *medicine* (or mystery).

The reader may here very properly inquire, If the American traditions of the Deluge have not been brought from the Eastern Continent, how is it that the Mandans have the Mosaic account of the olive-branch and the dove? This is easily explained; for these terms, and "Big Canoe," used by the Mandans, form no part of the general traditions, being entirely unused by, and unknown to, the other tribes of the American Continent; but have been introduced amongst the Mandans, like other customs that will be described, by some errant colony of Welsh, or other civilized people who have merged into the Mandan tribe, and, having witnessed the Mandan ceremonies, and heard their traditions of the Deluge, have described to those people the Mosaic account, and from which the Mandans have appropriated and introduced into their system the terms "willow-bough" for olive-branch, and "Big Canoe" for the Ark, whilst all the other tribes which speak of a canoe use the word *"canoe"* only. And there are yet many tribes in the vicinity of the Rocky Mountains, and in the north of Mexico, which, without impairing in the least the great fact of the tradition, make no mention of a canoe whatever, but represent that the ancestor or ancestors of the present human race, by various miraculous modes, which they describe, gained the summit of a mountain above the reach of the waters in which the rest of mankind perished.

In Plate II. I have given a bird's-eye view of a section of the Mandan village, which is necessary to enable the reader fully to understand the ceremonies to be described.[8]

As I have before said, these people all lived in one village, and their wigwams were covered with earth,—they were all of one form; the frames or shells constructed of timbers, and covered with a thatching of willow-boughs, and over and on that, with a foot or two in thickness, of a concrete of tough clay and gravel, which became so hard as to admit the whole group of inmates, with their dogs, to recline upon their tops. These wigwams varied in size from thirty to sixty feet in diameter, were perfectly round, and often contained from twenty to thirty persons within.

The village was well protected in front by a high and precipitous rocky bank of the river; and, in the rear, by a stockade of timbers firmly set in the ground, with a ditch inside, not for water, but for the protection of the warriors who occupied it when firing their arrows between the pickets.

In this view the *"Medicine Lodge,"* as it is termed, and the *"Big*

Canoe" (or symbol of the *"Ark"*) are conspicuous, and their positions should be borne in mind during the descriptions of the ceremonies that are to be given.

The *"Medicine Lodge,"* the largest in the village and seventy-five feet in diameter, with four images (sacrifices of different-coloured and costly cloths) suspended on poles above it, was considered by these people as a sort of temple, held as strictly sacred, being built and used solely for these four days' ceremonies, and closed during the rest of the year.

In an open area in the centre of the village stands the Ark (or *"Big Canoe"*), around which a great proportion of their ceremonies were performed. This rude symbol, of eight or ten feet in height, was constructed of planks and hoops, having somewhat the appearance of a large hogshead standing on its end, and containing some mysterious things which none but the *medicine men* were allowed to examine. An evidence of the sacredness of this object was the fact that though it had stood, no doubt for many years, in the midst and very centre of the village population, there was not the slightest dicoverable bruise or scratch upon it![9]

In the distance in this view, and outside of the picket, is seen a portion of their cemetery. Their dead, partially embalmed, are tightly wrapped in buffalo hides, softened with glue and water, and placed on slight scaffolds, above the reach of animals or human hands, each body having its separate scaffold.

The O-kee-pa, though in many respects apparently so unlike it, was strictly a *religious ceremony*, it having been conducted in most of its parts with the solemnity of religious worship, with abstinence, with sacrifices, and with prayer, whilst there were three other distinct and ostensible objects for which it was held.

1st. As an annual celebration of the event of the "subsiding of the waters" of the Deluge, of which they had a distinct tradition, and which in their language they called *"Mee-ne-ró-ka-há-sha"* (the settling down of the waters).

2nd. For the purpose of dancing what they called *"Bel-lohk-na-*

pick" (the bull-dance), to the strict performance of which they attributed the coming of buffaloes to supply them with food during the
ensuing year.

3rd. For the purpose of conducting the young men who had
arrived at the age of manhood during the past year, through an
ordeal of privation and bodily torture, which, while it was supposed
to harden their muscles and prepare them for extreme endurance,
enabled their chiefs, who were spectators of the scene, to decide upon
their comparative bodily strength, and ability to endure the priva-
tions and sufferings that often fall to the lot of Indian warriors, and
that they might decide who amongst the young men was the best
able to lead a war-party in an extreme exigency.[10]

The season having arrived for the holding of these ceremonies,
the leading *medicine* (mystery) man of the tribe presented himself
on the top of a wigwam one morning before sunrise, and haranguing
the people told them that "he discovered something very strange in
the western horizon, and he believed that at the rising of the sun
a great white man would enter the village from the west and open
the *Medicine Lodge.*"

In a few moments the tops of the wigwams, and all other eleva-
tions, were covered with men, women, and children on the look-out;
and at the moment the rays of the sun shed their first light over the
prairies and back of the village, a simultaneous shout was raised,
and in a few minutes all voices were united in yells and mournful
cries, and with them the barking and howling of dogs; all were in
motion and apparent alarm, preparing their weapons and securing
their horses, as if an enemy were rushing on them to take them by
storm.

All eyes were at this time directed to the prairie, where, at the
distance of a mile or so from the village, a solitary human figure was
seen descending the prairie hills and approaching the village in a
straight line, until he reached the picket, where a formidable array
of shields and spears was ready to receive him. A large body of
warriors was drawn up in battle-array, when their leader advanced

and called out to the stranger to make his errand known, and to tell from whence he came. He replied that he had come from the high mountains in the west, where he resided,—that he had come for the purpose of opening the *Medicine Lodge* of the Mandans, and that he must have uninterrupted access to it, or certain destruction would be the fate of the whole tribe.[11]

The head chief and the council of chiefs, who were at that moment assembled in the council-house, with their faces painted black, were sent for, and soon made their appearance in a body at the picket, and recognized the visitor as an old acquaintance, whom they addressed as *"Nu-mohk-múck-a-nah"* (the *first* or *only* man). All shook hands with him, and invited him within the picket. He then harangued them for a few minutes, reminding them that every human being on the surface of the earth had been destroyed by the water excepting himself, who had landed on a high mountain in the West, in his canoe, where he still resided, and from whence he had come to open the *Medicine Lodge,* that the Mandans might celebrate the subsiding of the waters and make the proper sacrifices to the water, lest the same calamity should again happen to them.

The next moment he was seen entering the village under the escort of the chiefs, when the cries and alarms of the villagers instantly ceased, and orders were given by the chiefs that the women and children should all be silent and retire within their wigwams, and their dogs all to be muzzled during the whole of that day, which belonged to the Great Spirit.

In the midst of this startling and thrilling scene, which was so well acted out by men, women, and children, and (apparently) by their dogs, I should scarcely have had the nerve to have been a close observer but for the announcement by the fur-trader, Mr. Kipp, with whom I was lodging, that this was the beginning of the "great ceremony," and that I ought not to lose a moment in witnessing its commencement, and of making sketches of all that transpired.

With this advice Mr. Kipp had accompanied me to the picket, where I had a fair view of the reception of this strange visitor from the West; in appearance a very aged man, whose body was naked, with the exception of a robe made of four white wolves' skins. His body and face and hair were entirely covered with white clay, and he closely resembled, at a little distance, a *centenarian* white man. In his left hand he extended, as he walked, a large pipe, which seemed to be borne as a very sacred thing. The procession moved to the *Medicine Lodge,* which this personage seemed to have the only means of opening. He opened it, and entered it alone, it having been (as I was assured) superstitiously closed during the past year, and never used since the last annual ceremony.

The chiefs then retired to the council-house, leaving this strange visitor sole tenant of this sacred edifice; soon after which he placed himself at its door, and called out to the chiefs to furnish him "four men,—one from the *North,* one from the *South,* one from the *East,* and one from the *West,* whose hands and feet were clean and would not profane the sacred temple while labouring within it during that day."

These four men were soon produced, and they were employed during the day in sweeping and cleaning every part of the temple, and strewing the floor, which was a concrete of gravel and clay, and ornamenting the sides of it, with willow-boughs and aromatic herbs which they gathered in the prairies, and otherwise preparing it for the *"Ceremonies,"* to commence on the next morning.

During the remainder of that day, while all the Mandans were shut up in their wigwams, and not allowed to go out, *Nu-mohk-múck-a-nah* (the *first* or *only* man) visited alone each wigwam, and, while crying in front of it, the owner appeared and asked, "Who's there?" and "What was wanting?" To this *Nu-mohk-múck-a-nah* replied by relating the destruction of all the human family by the *Flood,* excepting himself, who had been saved in his "Big Canoe," and now dwelt in the West; that he had come to open the *Medicine Lodge,* that the Mandans might make the necessary sacrifices to the water, and for this purpose it was requisite that he should receive at the door of every Mandan's wigwam some edged tool to be given to the water as a sacrifice, as it was with such tools that the *"Big Canoe"* was built.

He then demanded and received at the door of every Mandan wigwam, some edged or pointed tool or instrument made of iron or steel, which seemed to have been procured and held in readiness for the occasion; with these he returned to the *Medicine Lodge* at evening, where he deposited them, and where they remained during the four days of the ceremony, and were, as will be seen, on the last day at sundown, in the presence of the chiefs and all the tribe, to be thrown into deep water from the top of the rocks, and thus made a sacrifice to the water.[12]

Nu-mohk-múck-a-nah rested alone in the Medicine Lodge during that night, and at sunrise the next morning, in front of the lodge, called out for all the young men who were candidates for the O-kee-pa graduation as warriors, to come forward,—the rest of the villages still enclosed in their wigwams.

In a few minutes about fifty young men, who I learned were all of those of the tribe who had arrived at maturity during the last year, appeared in a beautiful group, their graceful limbs entirely denuded, but without exception covered with clay of different colours from head to foot,—some white, some red, some yellow, and others blue and green, each one carrying his shield of bull's hide on his left arm, and his bow in his left hand, and his *medicine-bag* in the right.[13]

In this plight they followed *Nu-mohk-múck-a-nah* into the Medicine Lodge in "Indian file," and taking their positions around the sides of the lodge, each one hung his bow and quiver, shield and *medicine-bag* over him as he reclined upon the floor of the wigwam.

Nu-mohk-múck-a-nah then called into the *Medicine Lodge* the principal *medicine man* of the tribe, whom he appointed *O-kee-pa-ka-see-ka* (Keeper or Conductor of the Ceremonies), by passing into his hand the large pipe which he had so carefully brought with him, "which had been saved in the big canoe with him," and on which it will appear the whole of these mysteries hung.[14]

Nu-mohk-múck-a-nah then took leave of him by shaking hands with him, and left the Medicine Lodge, saying that he would return to the West, where he lived, and be back again in just a year to re-open the Medicine Lodge. He then passed through the village, shaking hands with the chiefs, and in a few moments was seen disappearing over the hills from whence he came the day previous.

No more was *seen* of this extraordinary personage during the ceremonies, but more will be learned of him before this description is finished.*

Here is the proper place to relate the manner in which I gained admission into this sacred temple, and to give the credit that was due, to the man who kindly gave me permission to witness what was probably never seen before by a white man, the secret and sacred transactions of the interior of the Mandan Medicine Lodge, so sacred that a double door, with an intervening passage and an armed sentinel at each end, positively denying all access except by permission of the Conductor of the Ceremonies, and strictly guarding it against the approach or gaze of women, who, I was told, had never been allowed to catch the slightest glance of its interior.

This interior had also been too sacred a place for the admission of Mr. Kipp, the fur-trader, who had lived in the village eight or ten years; but luckily for me, I had completed a portrait the day before, of the renowned doctor or *"mystery man,"* to whom the superintendence of the ceremonies had just been committed, and whose vanity had been so much excited by the painting that he had mounted on to a wigwam with it, holding it up by the corners and haranguing the villagers, claiming that "he must be the greatest man among the Mandans, because I had painted his portrait before I had painted the great chief; and that I was the greatest *'medicine'*

---

*Here the question again arises, If the Indian tradition of the Deluge was not of Mosaic origin, why was the "first or only man" represented by the Mandans as a white man? and the answer is the same as that already given as to the "willow-bough" and the "big canoe." The same teachers have made these people believe that the first man was a *white* man, and they consequently so represent him,—a peculiarity of the Mandans, not practised or thought of in any other tribe of the American continent.

of the whites, and a great chief, because I could make so perfect a duplicate of him that it set all the women and children laughing!"[15]

This man, then, in charge of the Medicine Lodge, seeing me with one of my men and Mr. Kipp, the fur-trader, standing in front of the door, came out, and passing his arm through mine, politely led me into the lodge, and allowing my hired man and Mr. Kipp, with one of the clerks of his establishment, to follow. We took our seats, and were allowed to resume them on the three following days, occupying them most of the time from sunrise to sundown; and therefore the following description of those scenes, and the paintings which I then made of them, and to all of which Mr. Kipp and the other two men attached their certificates, are here given.

> We hereby certify that we witnessed, with Mr. Catlin, in the Mandan village, the ceremonies represented in the four paintings to which this certificate refers, and that he has therein represented those scenes as we saw them enacted, without addition or exaggeration.
>
> J. KIPP, *Agent of Missouri Fur Company.*
> J. CRAWFORD, *Clerk.*
> ABRAHAM BOGARD.

Mandan Village, 28*th July,* 1832.[16]

The Conductor or Master of the Ceremonies then took his position, reclining on the ground near the fire, in the centre of the lodge, with the medicine-pipe in his hand, and commenced crying, and continued to cry to the Great Spirit, while he guarded the young candidates who were reclining around the sides of the lodge, and for four days and four nights were not allowed to eat, drink, or to sleep. (This interior, which they called *"Mee-ne-ro-ka-Há-sha,"*—the waters settle down,—see in Plate III.)

By such denial great lassitude, and even emaciation, was produced, preparing the young men for the tortures which they afterwards went through.

The Medicine Lodge, in which they were thus resting during the four days, and which I have said was seventy-five feet in diameter, presented the most strange and picturesque appearance. Its sides were curiously decorated with willow-boughs and aromatic herbs, and its floor (covered also with willow-boughs) with a curious arrangement of buffalo and human skulls.[17]

There were also four articles of veneration and importance lying on the ground, which were sacks, containing each some three or four gallons of water. These seemed to be objects of great superstitious regard, and had been made with much labour and ingenuity, being constructed of the skins of the buffalo's neck, and sewed together in the forms of large tortoises lying on their backs, each having a sort of tail made of raven's quills, and a stick like a drumstick lying on it, with which, as will be seen in a subsequent part of the ceremony, the musicians beat upon the sacks as instruments of music for their strange dances.

By the sides of these sacks, which they called *Eeh-tee-ka* (drums), there were two other articles of equal importance, which they called *Eeh-na-de* (rattles), made of dried undressed skins, shaped into the form of gourd-shells, which they also used, as will be seen, as another part of the music for their dances.

The sacks of water had the appearance of great antiquity, and the Mandans pretended that the water had been contained in them ever since the Deluge. At what time it had been originally put in, or when replenished, I consequently could not learn. I made several efforts to purchase one of these tortoise drums, so elaborately and curiously were they embroidered and ornamented, offering them goods at the Fur Company's trading-house to the value of one hundred dollars, but they said they were *medicine* (mystery) things, and therefore could not be sold at any price.[18]

Such was the appearance of the interior of the Medicine Lodge during the three first (and part of the fourth) days. During the three first days, while things remained thus inside of the Medicine

Lodge, there were many curious and grotesque amusements and ceremonies transpiring outside and around the "Big Canoe."

The principal of these, which they called *Bel-lohk-na-pick* (the bull-dance), to the strict observance of which they attributed the coming of buffaloes to supply them with food, was one of an exceedingly grotesque and amusing character, and was danced four times on the first day, eight times on the second day, twelve times on the third day, and sixteen times on the fourth day, and always around the "Big Canoe," of which I have already spoken. (See the "Bull-Dance," Plate IV.)

The chief actors in these strange scenes were eight men, with the entire skins of buffaloes thrown over them, enabling them closely to imitate the appearance and motions of those animals, as the bodies of the dancers were kept in a horizontal position, the horns and tails of the animals remaining on the skins, and the skins of the animals' heads served as masks, through the eyes of which the dancers were looking.

The eight men were all naked and painted exactly alike, and in the most extraordinary manner; their bodies, limbs, and faces being everywhere covered with black, red, or white paint. Each joint was marked with two white rings, one within the other, even to the joints in the under jaw, the fingers and the toes; and the abdomens were painted to represent the face of an infant, the navel representing its mouth. (See "A Buffalo Bull," Plate V.*)

Each one of these characters also had a lock of buffalo's hair tied around the ankles, in his right hand a rattle (*she-shée-quoin*), and a slender staff six feet in length in the other; and carried on his back, above the buffalo skin, a bundle of willow-boughs, of the ordinary size of a bundle of wheat. (See "A Buffalo Bull" dancing, Plate VI.)[19]

---

*Whilst the handsome warrior was standing for the sketch here given, he told me that it took eight men an entire day to paint the bodies and limbs of the eight buffaloes, no part of the painting being done by their own hands.

These eight men representing eight buffalo bulls, being divided into four pairs, took their positions on the four sides of the Ark, or "Big Canoe" (as seen in the general view, Plate IV.), representing thereby the four cardinal points; and between each couple of these, with his back turned to the "Big Canoe," was another figure engaged in the same dance, keeping step with the eight buffalo bulls, with a staff in one hand and a rattle in the other: and being four in number, answered again to the four cardinal points.

The bodies of these four men were also entirely naked, with the exception of beautiful kilts of eagles' quills and ermine, and head-dresses made of the same materials.

Two of these figures were painted jet black with charcoal and grease, whom they called *the night,* and the numerous white spots dotted over their bodies and limbs they called *stars.* (See one of these, Plate VII.)

The other two, who were painted from head to foot as red as vermilion could make them, with white stripes up and down over their bodies and limbs, were called the *morning rays* (symbols of day). (See one of them, Plate VII.)[20]

These twelve were the only figures actually engaged in the Bull *dance,* which was each time repeated in the same manner without any apparent variation. There were, however, a great number of characters, many of them representing various animals of the country, engaged in giving the whole effect to this strange scene, and all of which are worthy of a few remarks.

The bull-dance was conducted by the old master of ceremonies (*O-kee-pa-ka-see-ka*) carrying his medicine pipe; his body entirely naked, and covered as well as his hair, with yellow clay.

For each time the bull-dance was repeated, this man came out of the Medicine Lodge with the *medicine pipe* in his hands, bringing with him four old men carrying the tortoise drums, their bodies painted red, and head-dresses of eagles' quills, and with them another old man with the two *she-shée-quoins* (rattles). These took their seats by the side of the "Big Canoe," and commenced drum-

ming and rattling and singing, whilst the conductor of the ceremonies, with his medicine pipe in his hands, was leaning against the
"Big Canoe," and crying in his full voice to the Great Spirit, as seen
in the general view, Plate IV. Squatted on the ground, on the opposite side of the "Big Canoe," were two men with skins of grizzly bears
thrown over them, using the skins as masks covering their faces.
Their bodies were naked, and painted with yellow clay.

These characters, whom they called *grizzly bears,* were continually
growling and threatening to devour everything before them, and
interfering with the forms of the ceremony. To appease them and
keep them quiet, the women were continually bringing and placing
before them dishes of meat, which were as often snatched away and
carried to the prairies by two men called *bald eagles,* whose bodies
and limbs were painted black, whilst their heads and feet and hands
were whitened with clay. These were again chased upon the prairies
by a numerous group of small boys, whose bodies and limbs were
painted yellow, and their heads white wearing tails of white deer's
hair, and whom they called *antelopes.*

Besides these there were two men representing *swans,* their bodies
naked and painted white, and their noses and feet were painted
black.

There were two men called *rattlesnakes,* their bodies naked and
curiously painted, resembling that reptile; each holding a rattle in
one hand and a bunch of wild sage in the other. (See "A Rattle-
snake," Plate VIII.) There were two *beavers,* represented by two
men entirely covered with dresses made of buffalo skins, except their
heads, and wearing beavers' tails attached to their belts. (See "A
Beaver," Plate VIII.)

There were two men representing *vultures,* their bodies naked
and painted brown, their heads and shoulders painted blue, and
their noses red.

Two men represented *wolves,* their bodies naked, wearing wolf-
skins. These pursued the antelopes, and whenever they overtook
one of them on the prairie one or both of the grizzly bears came up

Plate VIII.   Dancers Representing Snake and Beaver

Plate IX.   O-ke-hée-de, the Evil Spirit

Plate X. Torture Scene in the Medicine Lodge

Plate XI.   Young Men Undergoing Torture

and pretended to devour it, in revenge for the antelopes having devoured the meat given to the grizzly bears by the women.[21]

All these characters closely imitated the habits of the animals they represented, and they all had some peculiar and appropriate songs, which they constantly chanted and sang during the dances, without even themselves (probably) knowing the meaning of them, they being strictly *medicine songs,* which are kept profound secrets from those of their own tribe, except those who have been regularly initiated into their *medicines* (mysteries) at an early age, and at an exorbitant price; and I therefore failed to get a translation of them.

At the close of each of these bull-dances, these representatives of animals and birds all set up the howl and growl peculiar to their species, in a deafening chorus; some dancing, some jumping, and others (apparently) flying; the *beavers* clapping with their tails, the *rattlesnakes* shaking their rattles, the *bears* striking with their paws, the *wolves* howling, and the *buffaloes* rolling in the sand or rearing upon their hind feet; and dancing off together to an adjoining lodge, where they remained in a curious and picturesque group until the master of ceremonies came again out of the Medicine Lodge, and leaning as before against the "Big Canoe," cried out for all the dancers, musicians, and the group of animals and birds to gather again around him.

This lodge, which was also strictly a Medicine Lodge during the occasion, and used for painting and arranging all the characters, and not allowed to be entered during the four days, except by the persons taking part in the ceremonies, was shown to me by the conductor of the ceremonies, who sent a *medicine man* with me to its interior whilst the scene of painting and ornamenting their bodies for the *bull-dance* was taking place; and none but the most vivid imagination could ever conceive anything so peculiar, so wild, and so curious in effect as this strange spectacle then presented to my view.

No man painted himself, but, standing or lying naked, submitted like a statue to the operations of other hands, who were appointed for the purpose. Each painter seemed to have his special department or peculiar figure, and each appeared to be working with great care and with ambition for the applause of the public when he turned out his figure.

It may be thought easy to imagine such a group of naked figures, and the effect that the rude painting on their bodies would have; but I am ready to declare that the most creative imagination cannot appreciate the singular beauty of these graceful figures thus decorated with various colours, reclining in groups, or set in rapid motion; it was one of those few scenes that must be witnessed to be fully appreciated.

The first ordeal they all went through in this sanctuary was that of *Tah-ke-way ka-ra-ka* (the hiding man), the name given to an aged man, who was supplied with small thongs of deer's sinew, for the purpose of obscuring the *glans* secret, which was uniformly done by this operator, with all the above-named figures, by drawing the prepuce over in front of the glans, and tying it secure with the sinew, and then covering the private parts with clay, which he took from a wooden bowl, and, with his hand, plastered unsparingly over.

Of men performing their respective parts in the *bull-dance,* representing the various animals, birds, and reptiles of the country, there were about forty, and forty boys representing antelopes,— making a group in all of eighty figures, entirely naked, and painted from head to foot in the most fantastic shapes, and of all colours, as has been described; and the fifty young men resting in the Medicine Lodge, and waiting for the infliction of their tortures, were also naked and entirely covered with clay of various colours (as has been described), some red, some yellow, and others blue and green; so that of (probably) one hundred and thirty persons engaged in these picturesque scenes, *not one single inch of the natural colour of their bodies, their limbs, or their hair could be seen!*[22]

During each and every one of these bull-dances, the four old men who were beating on the sacks of water, were chanting forth their supplications to the Great Spirit for the continuation of his favours, in sending them buffaloes to supply them with food for the ensuing year. They were also exciting the courage and fortitude of the young men inside of the Medicine Lodge, who were listening to their prayers, by telling them that "the Great Spirit had opened his ears in their behalf; that the very atmosphere out-of-doors was full of peace and happiness for them when they got through; that the women and children could hold the mouths and paws of the grizzly bears; that they had invoked from day to day the Evil Spirit; that they were still challenging him to come, and yet he had not dared to make his appearance."

But, in the midst of the last dance on the fourth day, a sudden alarm throughout the group announced the arrival of a strange character from the West. Women were crying, dogs were howling, and all eyes were turned to the prairie, where, a mile or so in distance, was seen an individual man making his approach towards the village; his colour was black, and he was darting about in different directions, and in a zigzag course approached and entered the village, amidst the greatest (apparent) imaginable fear and consternation of the women and children.

This strange and frightful character, whom they called *O-ke-hée-de* (the owl or Evil Spirit), darted through the crowd where the buffalo-dance was proceeding (as seen in Plate IV.), alarming all he came in contact with. His body was painted jet black with pulverized charcoal and grease, with rings of white clay over his limbs and body. Indentations of white, like huge teeth, surrounded his mouth, and white rings surrounded his eyes. In his two hands he carried a sort of wand—a slender rod of eight feet in length, with a red ball at the end of it, which he slid about upon the ground as he ran. (See "O-ke-hée-de," Plate IX.)

On entering the crowd where the buffalo-dance was going on, he directed his steps towards the groups of women, who retreated in the greatest alarm, tumbling over each other and screaming for help as he advanced upon them. At this moment of increased alarm the screams of the women had brought by his side *O-kee-pa-ka-see-ka* (the conductor of the ceremonies) with his medicine pipe, for their protection. This man had left the "Big Canoe," against which he was leaning and crying during the dance, and now thrust his *medi-cine* pipe before this hideous monster, and, looking him full in the eyes, held him motionless under its *charm,* until the women and children had withdrawn from his reach.

The awkwardness of the position of this blackened demon, and the laughable appearance of the two, frowning each other in the face, while the women and children and the whole crowd were laughing at them, were amusing beyond the power of description.

After a round of hisses and groans from the crowd, and the women had retired to a safe distance, the *medicine* pipe was grad-ually withdrawn, and this vulgar monster, whose wand was slowly lowering to the ground, gained power of locomotion again.

The conductor of the ceremonies returned to the "Big Canoe," and resumed his former position and crying, as the buffalo-dance was still proceeding, without interruption.

The Evil Spirit in the meantime had wandered to another part of the village, where the screams of the women were again heard, and the conductor of the ceremonies again ran with the medicine pipe in his hands to their rescue, and arriving just in time, and holding this monster in check as before, enabled them again to escape.

In several attempts of this kind the Evil Spirit was thus defeated, after which he came wandering back amongst the dancers, apparent-ly much fatigued and disappointed; and the women gradually ad-vancing and gathering around him, evidently less apprehensive of danger than a few moments before.

In this *distressing* dilemma he was approached by an old matron, who came up slily behind him with both hands full of yellow dirt, which (by reaching around him) she suddenly dashed in his face, covering him from head to foot and changing his colour, as the dirt adhered to the undried bears'-grease on his skin. As he turned around he received another handful, and another, from different quarters; and at length another snatched his wand from his hands, and broke it across her knee; others grasped the broken parts, and, snapping them into small bits, threw them into his face. His power was thus gone, and his colour changed: he began then to cry, and, bolting through the crowd, he made his way to the prairies, where he fell into the hands of a fresh swarm of women and girls (no doubt assembled there for the purpose) outside of the picket, who hailed him with screams and hisses and terms of reproach, whilst they were escorting him for a considerable distance over the prairie, and beating him with sticks and dirt.

He was at length seen escaping from this group of women, who were returning to the village, whilst he was disappearing over the plains from whence he had made his first appearance.

The crowd of women entered the village, and the area where the ceremony was transpiring, in triumph, and the fortunate one who had deprived him of his power was escorted by two matrons on each side. She was then lifted by her four female attendants on to the front of the Medicine Lodge, directly over its door, where she stood and harangued the multitude for some time; claiming that "she held the power of *creation,* and also the power of life and death over them; that she was the father of all the buffaloes, and that she could make them come or stay away, as she pleased."

She then ordered the bull-dance to be stopped—the four musicians to carry the four tortoise-drums into the Medicine Lodge. The assistant dancers, and all the other characters taking parts, were ordered into the dressing and painting lodge. The buffalo and human skulls on the floor of the Medicine Lodge (as seen in Plate III.) she ordered to be hung on the four posts (as seen in Plate X.). She invited the chiefs to enter the Medicine Lodge, and (being seated) to witness the voluntary tortures of the young men, now to commence. She ordered the conductor of the ceremonies to sit by the fire and smoke the *medicine* pipe, and the operators to go in with their knife and splints, and to commence the tortures.

She then called out for and demanded the handsomest woman's dress in the Mandan village, which was due to her who had disarmed *O-ke-hée-de* and had the power of making all the buffaloes which the

Mandans would require during the coming year. Her demand for this beautiful dress was *peremptory,* and she must have it to lead the dance in the *Feast of the Buffaloes,* to be given that night.

The beautiful dress was then presented to her by the conductor of the ceremonies, who said to her, "Young woman, you have gained great fame this day; and the honour of leading the dance in the *Feast of the Buffaloes,* to be given this night, belongs to you."

Thus ended the bull-dance (*Bel-lohk-na-pick*) and other amusements at midday on the fourth day of the O-kee-pa, preparatory to the scenes of torture to take place in the Medicine Lodge; and the pleasing *moral* from these strange (and in some respects disgusting) modes, at once suggests itself, that in the midst of their religious ceremony the Evil Spirit had made his *entrée* for the purpose of doing mischief, and, having been defeated in all his designs by the magic power of the medicine pipe, on which all those ceremonies hung, he had been disarmed and driven out of the village in disgrace by the very part of the community he came to impose upon.[23]

The *bull-dance* and other grotesque scenes being finished outside of the Medicine Lodge, the torturing scene (or *pohk-hong* as they called it) commenced within, in the following manner. (See Plate X.)

The young men reclining around the sides of the Medicine Lodge (before shown in Plate III.), who had now reached the middle of the fourth day without eating, drinking, or sleeping, and consequently weakened and emaciated, commenced to submit to the operation of the knife and other instruments of torture.

Two men, who were to inflict the tortures, had taken their positions near the middle of the lodge; one, with a large knife with a sharp point and two edges, which were hacked with another knife in order to produce as much pain as possible, was ready to make the incisions through the flesh, and the other, prepared with a handful of splints of the size of a man's finger, and sharpened at both ends, to be passed through the wounds as soon as the knife was withdrawn.

The bodies of these two men, who were probably *medicine men,* were painted red, with their hands and feet black; and the one who made the incisions with the knife wore a mask, that the young men should never know who gave them their wounds; and on their bodies and limbs they had conspicuously marked with paint the scars which they bore, as evidence that they had passed through the same ordeal.

To these two men one of the emaciated candidates at a time crawled up, and submitted to the knife (as seen in Plate X.), which was passed under and through the integuments and flesh taken up between the thumb and forefinger of the operator, on each arm, above and below the elbow, over the *brachialis externus* and the *extensor radialis,* and on each leg above and below the knee, over the *vastus externus* and the *peroneus;* and also on each breast and each shoulder.

During this painful operation, most of these young men, as they took their position to be operated upon, observing me taking notes, beckoned me to look them in the face, and sat, without the apparent change of a muscle, smiling at me whilst the knife was passing through their flesh, the ripping sound of which, and the trickling of blood over their clay-covered bodies and limbs, filled my eyes with irresistible tears.

When these incisions were all made, and the splints passed through, a cord of raw hide was lowered down through the top of the wigwam, and fastened to the splints on the breasts or shoulders, by which the young man was to be raised up and suspended, by men placed on the top of the lodge for the purpose.

These cords having been attached to the splints on the breast or the shoulders, each one had his shield hung to some one of the splints: his *medicine bag* was held in his left hand, and a dried buffalo skull was attached to the splint on each lower leg and each lower arm, that its weight might prevent him from struggling; when, at a signal, by striking the cord, the men on top of the lodge commenced to draw him up. He was thus raised some three or four feet above the ground, until the buffalo heads and other articles attached to the wounds swung clear, when another man, his body red and

his hands and feet black, stepped up, and, with a small pole, began
to turn him around.

The turning was low at first, and gradually increased until fainting ensued, when it ceased. In each case these young men submitted
to the knife, to the insertion of the splints, and even to being hung
and lifted up, without a perceptible murmur or a groan; but when
the turning commenced, they began crying in the most heartrending
tones to the Great Spirit; imploring him to enable them to bear
and survive the painful ordeal they were entering on. This piteous
prayer, the sounds of which no imagination can ever reach, and of
which I could get no translation, seemed to be an established form,
ejaculated alike by all, and continued until fainting commenced,
when it gradually ceased.

In each instance they were turned until they fainted and their
cries were ended. Their heads hanging forwards and down, and their
tongues distended, and becoming entirely motionless and silent,
they had, in each instance, the appearance of a corpse. (See Plate XI.)
In this view, which was sketched whilst the two young men were
hanging before me, one is suspended by the muscles of the breast,
and the other by the muscles of the shoulders, and two of the young
candidates are seen reclining on the ground, and waiting for their
turn.

When brought to this condition, without signs of animation, the
lookers-on pronounced the word *dead! dead!* when the men who
had turned them struck the cords with their poles, which was the
signal for the men on top of the lodge to lower them to the ground,
—the time of their suspension having been from fifteen to twenty
minutes.

The excessive pain produced by the turning, which was evinced
by the increased cries as the rapidity of the turning increased, was
no doubt caused by the additional weight of the buffalo skulls upon
the splints, in consequence of their centrifugal direction, caused by
the rapidity with which the bodies were turned, added to the sicken-
ing distress of the rotary motion; and what that double agony ac-

tually was, every adult Mandan knew, and probably no human being but a Mandan ever felt.

After this ordeal (in which two or three bodies were generally hanging at the same time), and the bodies were lowered to the ground as has been described, a man advanced (as is seen in Plate X.) and withdrew the two splints by which they had been hung up, they having necessarily been passed under a portion of the *trapezius* or *pectoral* muscle, in order to support the weight of their bodies; but leaving all the others remaining in the flesh, to be got rid of in the manner yet to be described.

Each body lowered to the ground appeared like a loathsome and lifeless corpse. No one was allowed to offer them aid whilst they lay in this condition. They were here enjoying their inestimable privilege of voluntarily entrusting their lives to the keeping of the Great Spirit, and chose to remain there until the Great Spirit gave them strength to get up and walk away.

In each instance, as soon as they got strength enough *partly* to rise, and move their bodies to another part of the lodge, where there sat a man with a hatchet in his hand and a dried buffalo skull before him, his body red, his hands and feet black, and wearing a mask, they held up the little finger of the left hand (as seen in Plate X.) towards the Great Spirit (offering it as a sacrifice, as they thanked him audibly, for having listened to their prayers and protected their lives in what they had just gone through), and laid it on the buffalo skull, where the man with the mask, struck it off at a blow with the hatchet, close to the hand.

In several instances I saw them offer immediately after, and give, the *fore*finger of the same hand,—leaving only the two middle fingers and the thumb to hold the bow, the only weapon used in that hand. Instances had been known, and several such were subsequently shown to me amongst the chiefs and warriors, where they had given also the little finger of the *right* hand, a much greater sacrifice; and several famous men of the tribe were also shown to me, who proved, by the corresponding scars on their breasts and limbs, which they exhibited to me, that they had been several times, at their own option, through these horrid ordeals.[24]

The young men seemed to take no care or notice of the wounds thus made, and neither bleeding nor inflammation to any extent ensued, though arteries were severed,—owing probably to the checked circulation caused by the reduced state to which their four days and nights of fasting and other abstinence had brought them.

During the whole time of this cruel part of the ceremonies, the chiefs and other dignitaries of the tribe were looking on, to decide who amongst the young men were the hardiest and stoutest-hearted, who could hang the longest by his torn flesh without fainting, and who was soonest up after he had fainted,—that they might decide whom to appoint to lead a war party, or to place at the most important posts, in time of war.

As soon as six or eight had passed through the ordeal as above described, they were led out of the Medicine Lodge, with the weights still hanging to their flesh and dragging on the ground, to undergo another and (perhaps) still more painful mode of suffering.

This part of the ceremony, which they called *Eeh-ke-náh-ka Na-pick* (the last race) (see Plate XII.), took place in presence of the whole tribe, who were lookers-on. For this a circle was formed by the buffalo-dancers (their masks thrown off) and others who had taken parts in the bull-dance, now wearing head-dresses of eagles' quills, and all connected by circular wreaths of willow-boughs held in their hands, who ran, with all possible speed and piercing yells, around the "Big Canoe"; and outside of that circle the bleeding young men thus led out, with all their buffalo skulls and other weights hanging to the splints, and dragging on the ground, were placed at equal distances, with two athletic young men assigned to each, one on each side, their bodies painted one half red and the other blue, and carrying a bunch of willow-boughs in one hand (see one of them, Plate XIII.), who took them, by leather straps fastened to the wrists, and ran with them as fast as they could, around the "Big Canoe"; the buffalo skulls and other weights still dragging on the ground as they ran, amidst the deafening shouts of the by-standers and the runners in the inner circle, who raised their voices to the highest key, to drown the cries of the poor fellows thus suffering by the violence of their tortures.

The ambition of the young aspirants in this part of the ceremony was to decide who could run the longest under these circumstances without fainting, and who could be soonest on his feet again after having been brought to that extremity. So much were they exhausted, however, that the greater portion of them fainted and settled down before they had run half the circle, and were then violently dragged, even (in some cases) with their faces in the dirt, until every weight attached to their flesh was left behind.

This *must* be done to produce honourable scars, which could not be effected by withdrawing the splints endwise; the flesh must be *broken out,* leaving a scar an inch or more in length: and in order to do this, there were several instances where the buffalo skulls adhered so long that they were jumpd upon by the bystanders as they were being dragged at full speed, which forced the splints out of the wounds by breaking the flesh, and the buffalo skulls were left behind.

The tortured youth, when thus freed from all weights, was left upon the ground, appearing like a mangled corpse, whilst his two torturers, having dropped their willow-boughs, were seen running through the crowd towards the prairies, as if to escape the punishment that would follow the commission of a heinous crime.

In this pitiable condition each sufferer was left, his life again entrusted to the keeping of the Great Spirit, the sacredness of which privilege no one had a right to infringe upon by offering a helping hand. Each one in his turn lay in this condition until "the Great Spirit gave him strength to rise upon his feet," when he was seen, covered with marks of trickling blood, staggering through the crowd and entering his wigwam, where his wounds were probably dressed, and with food and sleep his strength was restored.

The chiefs and other dignitaries of the tribe were all spectators here also, deciding who amongst the young men were the strongest, and could run the longest in the *last race* without fainting, and whom to appoint and promote accordingly.[25]

As soon as the six or eight thus treated were off from the ground, as many more were led out of the Medicine Lodge and passed through the same ordeal, or took some other more painful mode, at their own option, to rid themselves of the splints and weights attached to their limbs, until the whole number of candidates were disposed of; and on the occasion I am describing, to the whole of which I was a spectator, I should think that about fifty suffered in succession, and in the same manner.

The number of wounds inflicted required to be the same on each, and the number of weights attached to them the same, but in both stages of the torture the candidates had their choice of being, in the *first,* suspended by the breasts or by the shoulders; and in the *"last race"* of being dragged as has been described, or to wander about the prairies from day to day, and still without food, until suppuration of the wounds took place, and, by the decay of the flesh, the dragging weights were left behind.

It was natural for me to inquire, as I did, whether any of these young men ever died in the extreme part of this ceremony, and they could tell me of but one instance within their recollection, in which case the young man was left for three days upon the ground (unapproached by his relatives or by physicians) before they were quite certain that the Great Spirit did not intend to help him away. They all seemed to speak of this, however, as an enviable fate rather than as a misfortune; for "the Great Spirit had so willed it for some especial purpose, and no doubt for the young man's benefit."[26]

After the Medicine Lodge had thus been cleared of its tortured inmates, the master or conductor of ceremonies returned to it alone, and, gathering up the edged tools which I have said were deposited there, and to be sacrificed to the water on the last day of the ceremony, he proceeded to the bank of the river, accompanied by all the tribe, in whose presence, and with much form and ceremony, he sacrificed them by throwing them into deep water from the rocks, from which they could never be recovered: and then announced that the Great Spirit must be thanked by all—and that the O-kee-pa (religious ceremony of the Mandans) was finished.[27]

The *sequel* to this strange affair, and which has been briefly alluded to, and is yet to be described, was the

"FEAST OF THE BUFFALOES."

At the defeat of *O-ke-hée-de* (the Evil Spirit) it will be remembered that the young woman who returned from the prairie bearing the singular prize, and who ascended the front of the Medicine Lodge and put an end to the *bull-dance,* claimed the privilege of a beautiful dress, in which she was to lead the dance in the *feast of the buffaloes* on that night.

The O-kee-pa having been ended, and night having approached, several old men with rattles in their hands, which they were violently shaking, perambulated the village in various directions in the character of *criers,* announcing that "the whole government of the Mandans was then in the hands of one woman—she who had disarmed the Evil Spirit, and to whom they were to look during the coming year for buffaloes to supply them with food, and keep them alive; that all must repair to their wigwams and not show themselves outside; that the chiefs on that night were old women; that they had nothing to say; that no one was allowed to be out of their wigwams excepting the favoured ones whom *Rah-ta-co-puk-chee* (the governing woman) had invited to be at the *feast of the buffaloes* around the 'Big Canoe,' and which was about to commence."

This select party, which assembled and was seated on the ground in a circle, and facing the "Big Canoe," consisted (*first*) of the eight men who had danced the bull-dance, with the paint washed off. To them strictly the feast was given, and therefore was the *feast of the buffaloes* (and not to be confounded with the *buffalo feast,* another annual ceremony, given in the fall of the year, somewhat of a similar character, but held for a different purpose).

Besides the eight buffaloes were the old *medicine man,* conductor of the ceremonies, the four old men who had beaten on the tortoise-drums, and the one who had shaken the rattles, as musicians, and several of the aged chiefs of the tribe; and, added to these, this new-made, but temporary governess of the tribe, had invited some eight or ten of the young married women of the village, like herself, to pay the extraordinary *respect* that was due, by the custom of their country, to the makers of buffaloes and to reverenced old age on this extraordinary occasion.

The commencement of the ceremonies which fell under this woman's peculiar management was the *feast of the buffaloes* (as all the men invited to it were called *buffaloes*), which was handed around in wooden bowls by herself and attendants. After this was done, which lasted but a few minutes (appearing but a minor part of the affair), she charged a large pipe, which was passed around amongst the men, during which a lascivious dance was performed by herself and female companions.

This dance finished, she advanced to her first selected paramour, and, giving some signals which seemed to be understood, passed her hand gently under his arm, and, raising him up, led him through the village and into the prairie, where, as all the villagers and their dogs were shut up in their wigwams, they were free from observation or molestation.*

From this excursion they returned separately, and the man took his seat again if he chose to be a candidate for further civilities, or returned to his wigwam. The other women were singing and going through the whirl of the dance in the meantime, and each one inviting her chosen paramour, when she was disposed, in the same manner.

---

*In the foregoing account of the religious ceremonies, nothing has been described but what I saw enacted. Here, from necessity, I am trusting to the accounts of Mr. Kipp, of the Fur Company, and Mr. Tilton, whose letter will be seen in the Appendix, both of whom told me they had repeatedly been invited guests and sharers of these extraordinary hospitalities.

Those of the women who returned from these excursions joined again in the continuous dance, and extended as many and as varied invitations in this way as they desired; and some of them, I learned, as well as of the men, had taken several of such promenades in the course of the evening, which may be accounted for by the relieving fact that though it would have been a most prejudicial want of gallantry on the part of the man to have refused to go, yet the trifling present of a string of beads or an awl saved him from any odium which might otherwise have been cast upon him.

This extraordinary scene gradually closed by the men returning from the prairie to their homes, the last of them on the ground pacifying any unsatisfied feelings there might have been, by bestowing liberal presents amongst those women, and agreeing to smoke the pipe of friendship with their husbands the next day, which they were bound to offer, and the others, by the custom of the country, were bound to accept.

It may be met as matter of surprise, that a *religious ceremony* should be followed by a scene like the one just described, but before we entirely condemn these ignorant and superstitious people, let us inquire whether it is not, more or less, an inherent propensity in human nature (and even practised in some enlightened and Christian communities) to end extreme sorrow, extreme penitence, and even mourning for kindred the most loved, in *debauch?*[28]

What has thus far been related has been simple and easy, as it has been but the description of what I *saw* and what I *heard;* but what may be *expected* of me—rational and conclusive deductions from the above premises—I approach with timidity; rather wishing to submit the materials for the conclusions of others abler than myself to explain them, and for whose assistance I will still continue a few suggestions.

That the Mandans should have had a tradition of a *"Deluge"* is by no means singular, when in every tribe I have visited I have found that they regard some high mountain in their vicinity, on which, they say, their ancestor or ancestors were saved, and also relate other vague stories of the destruction of everything else living on the earth, by the waters.

But that these people should hold an annual celebration of that event, and that the season of the year for that celebration was decided by such circumstances as the "willow-bough" and its "full-grown leaves," and the *"medicine bird,"* and the Medicine Lodge opened by such a man as *"Nu-mohk-múck-a-nah,"* who represented a white man, and some other circumstances, is surely a very remarkable thing, and, as I think, deserves some further attention.

This *"Nu-mohk-múck-a-nah"* (first or only man) was undoubtedly some very aged *medicine man* of the tribe, who had gone out upon the prairies on the previous evening, and having dressed and painted himself for the occasion, came into the village at sunrise in the morning, endeavouring to keep up the semblance of reality; for the traditions of the Mandans say, that "at an ancient period such a man did actually come from the West, that his skin was white, that he was very old, that he appeared in all respects as has been represented; and, as has also been stated, that he related the manner of the destruction of every human being on the earth's surface by the waters, excepting himself, who was saved in his *"Big Canoe"* by landing on a high mountain in the West; that the Mandans and all other nations were his descendants, and were bound to make annual sacrifices of edged tools to the water, for with such things his "Big Canoe" was built; that he instructed the Mandans how to make their Medicine Lodge, and taught them also the forms of these annual ceremonies, and told them also that as long as they made these annual sacrifices and performed these rites to the full letter, they would be the favoured people of the Great Spirit, and would always have enough to eat and drink, and that so soon as they departed in the least degree from these forms their race would begin to decrease and finally die out.

These superstitious people have, no doubt, been living from time immemorial under the dread of such an injunction, and in the fear

Plate XII. The Last Race

Plate XIII.   Assistant to a Participant in the Last Race

of departing from it; and as they were living in total ignorance of its origin, other than this vague tradition, the world will probably remain in equal ignorance of much of its meaning, as they needs must be of all Indian traditions, which soon run into fable, thereby losing much of their system by which they might more easily have been correctly construed.

It would seem from their tradition of the willow-bough and the dove, that these people must have had some proximity to some part of the civilized world, or that missionaries or others had been amongst them teaching the Christian religion and the Mosaic account of the *Deluge,* which is in this and some other respects very different from the theories which all the other American tribes have distinctly established of that event.

There are other strong, and I think almost conclusive proofs, in support of this suggestion, which are to be drawn from the diversity of colour in their hair and complexions, as well as from their traditions just related of the "first or only man," whose body was white, and who came from the West, telling them of the destruction of the human race by the water; and in addition to the above I will offer another tradition, related to me by one of the chiefs of the tribe in the following way:—

"At a very ancient time *O-ke-hée-de* (the Evil Spirit) came from the West to the Mandan village in company with *Nu-mohk-múck-a-nah* (the first or only man), and they, being fatigued, sat down upon the ground near a woman who had but one eye and was hoeing corn. Her daughter, who was very beautiful, came up to her, and the Evil Spirit desired her to go and bring some water, but wished that before she started she would come to him and eat some buffalo meat.

"He then told her to take a piece out of his side, which she did, and ate it, and it proved to be buffalo's fat. She then went for the water, which she brought, and met them in the village where they had walked, and they both drank of it; nothing more was done. The friends of the girl soon after endeavoured to disgrace her by telling her that she was with child, which she did not deny. She declared at the same time her innocence, and boldly defied any man in the Mandan nation to come forward and accuse her. No one could accuse her, and she therefore became great 'medicine,' and she soon after went to the little Mandan village, where the child was born.

"Great search was made for her before she was found, as it was expected that the child also would be great 'medicine,' and in some way be of great importance to the tribe. They were induced to this belief from the strange manner of its conception and birth, and were soon confirmed in their belief from the wonderful things which it did at an early age.

"Amongst the strange things which it did on an occasion when the Mandans were in danger of starving, this child gave them four buffalo bulls, which filled the bellies of the whole nation, leaving as much meat as there was before they began to eat, and saying also that these four bulls would supply them for ever.

"*Nu-mohk-múck-a-nah* (the first or only man) was bent on the destruction of this child, and after making many fruitless searches for it, found it hidden in a dark place, and put it to death by throwing it into the river.

"When *O-ke-hée-de* (the Evil Spirit) heard of the death of this child, he sought for *Nu-mohk-múck-a-nah* with intent to kill him. He traced him a long distance, and at length overtook him at the Heart River, seventy miles below the Mandan village, with the '*big medicine pipe*' in his hands, the charm or mystery of which protected him from all his enemies. They soon agreed however to become good friends, and after smoking the *medicine pipe* they returned together to the Mandan village.

"The Evil Spirit was now satisfied, and *Nu-mohk-múck-a-nah* told the Mandans never to go beyond the mouth of Heart River to live, for it was the centre of the world, and to live beyond it would be destruction to them, and he named it *Nat-com-pa-sá-ha* (the heart or centre of the world)."[29]

Such was one of the very vague and imperfect traditions of those curious people, and I leave it to the world to judge of its similitude to the Scripture account of the Christian advent.

Omitting in this place their numerous other traditions and superstitions, I will barely refer to a few singular *deductions* I have made from the customs which have been described, and leave them for the consideration of gentlemen abler than myself to decide upon their importance.

The Mandans believed that the earth rests on the backs of *four* tortoises. They say that "each tortoise rained ten days, making forty days in all, and the waters covered the earth."

Whenever a Mandan doctor (*medicine man*) lighted his pipe, he invariably presented the stem of it to the north, the south, the east, and the west, the *four* cardinal points, and then upwards to the Great Spirit, before smoking it himself.

Their annual religious ceremony lasted *four* days; *four* men were called for by *Nu-mohk-múck-a-nah*, as has been stated, to cleanse and prepare the Medicine Lodge, "one from the north, one from the south, one from the east, and one from the west." *Four* was the number of tortoise-drums on the floor of the Medicine Lodge; there were also *four* buffalo and *four* human skulls arranged on the floor of the Medicine Lodge. There were *four* couples of dancers in the bull-dance, and *four* intervening dancers in the same dance, as has been described; the bull-dance was repeated *four* times on the first day, eight times on the second day, twelve times on the third day, and sixteen times on the fourth day, adding *four* dances on each of the four days, which added together make forty, the exact number of days that it rained upon the earth to produce the Deluge.

There were *four* sacrifices of various-coloured cloths raised on poles over the Medicine Lodge. The visits of *O-ke-hée-de* were paid to *four* of the buffaloes in the bull-dance; and in every instance of the young men who underwent the tortures explained, there were *four* splints run through the flesh on the legs, *four* on the arms, *four* on the body, and *four* buffalo-skulls attached to each one's wounds. And, as has been related in the tradition above given, *four* was the number of bulls given by the medicine child to feed the Mandans when they were starving.[30]

Such were a portion, but not all, of the *peculiar* modes of the hospitable and friendly Mandans, who have ceased to exist, and left almost the only tangible evidence of their having existed, in my collection, which contains their portraits, their manufactures, and all their modes, and which I hope to preserve with success for the information of ages to come.

The melancholy fate of these people was caused by the introduction of the smallpox, by that nefarious system of traffic which rapidly increases the wealth of civilized individual adventurers and monopolies who introduce it, but everywhere carries dissipation, poverty, disease and death to the poor Indians.

In the fourth summer after I left the Mandans, the Missouri Fur Company's steamer from St. Louis, freighted with whiskey and merchandise, and with two of the partners of that concern on board, moored at the shore of the river in front of the Mandan village, where a traffic was carried on with those unsuspecting people whilst there were two of the vessel's hands on board sick with the smallpox!

By this act of imprudence, and in fact of inhuman cruelty, the disease was communicated to those unfortunate people; and such were its awful results, with the self-destruction which ensued, that in the short space of three months there were but thirty-two of these people left in existence, with the exception of a few who had intermarried and were living with the *Minatarrees,* a friendly and neighbouring tribe.

A few months after the disease had subsided, the *Riccarrees,* a hostile tribe, living two hundred miles below, on the bank of the same river, moved up and took possession of the Mandan village, it being a better built town than their own, and by the side of the Fur Company's factory, making slaves of the remaining Mandans, who were unable to resist.

Whilst living in this condition in the Mandan village, and but a few months after they had taken possession, the Riccarrees were attacked by a war-party of Sioux, and in the midst of a desperate battle around the pickets, in which the remaining Mandans were taking a part, they suddenly, at a signal, passed through the pickets and threw themselves under the horses' feet of the Sioux, and were slain at their own seeking, rather than to live, as they said, "dogs of the Riccarrees."

My authorities for these painful facts are letters which I hold from Mr. K. M'Kenzie and Mr. J. Potts, written *in the Mandan village* after the disease had subsided. Both of these gentlemen were from Edinburgh, in Scotland, the former a partner in the Missouri Fur Company, and the latter a clerk in the same Company. (See these letters in Nos. 3 and 4 in the Appendix.)[31]

REMARKS.

In contemplating so many striking peculiarities in an extinguished tribe, the mind reluctantly leaves so interesting a subject without raising the question as to the origin of the people; and in this feeling, thought not within the original intention of this work, it is difficult for me to leave the subject without advancing my belief, and furnishing some part of my reasons for it, that many of the modes of these people were purely Welsh, and that the personal appearance and customs of the Mandans had been affected by the proximity or admixture of some wandering colony of Welsh who had been thrown at an early period somewhere upon the American coast.

I am here, perhaps, advancing a startling problem, which demands at my hands some striking proofs, which I will in a few words endeavour to produce.

The annual religious ceremony which has been described certainly cannot be attributed to the Welsh, nor am I able to compare it to any civilized custom, and I leave it for the world to decide whether it bears a resemblance to any known customs of savage or civilized races in other parts of the world.

It is very strange, as I have before said, that those people should have been instructed how to hold those ceremonies by a white man, and that they should be commenced and the Medicine Lodge opened by a white man, and that the "big canoe" should have been built with edged tools, if they be solely of native origin; and it would be equally or more strange if the Jesuit missionaries, who, it would seem, were the only civilized teachers we can well suppose to have reached these people, had instructed them in modes like those, though it is easy to believe that their teaching might have been the cause of the last singular tradition mentioned, certainly bearing a visible but very imperfect parallel to the Christian Advent.

Many of the customs and traditions of the western tribes convince us that those indefatigable preachers penetrated much further into the American wildernesses than history has followed them, and in this singular tribe we find the extraordinary custom which has been described, and others to which I shall take a few moments to allude, neither of which can with any propriety be attributed to the teaching of those venerable missionaries.

On my arrival in their village, my first glance amongst the Mandans forced me, from their peculiar features and complexions, the colour of their eyes and hair, the singular mode of building and furnishing their wigwams, etc., to believe that they were an amalgam of some foreign with an American aboriginal stock, and every day that I dwelt amongst them furnished me additional convictions of this fact, and of course called on my part for greater endeavours to account for these singularities. And the information I gathered amongst them confirmed me in the opinion I have advanced,—that many of their peculiarities and customs were Welsh, and therefore that there existed amongst them the remains of some Welsh colony, however difficult it might be to account for their having got there.

The following, I believe, will be received as interesting and important facts, and if they fail to establish my theory, they may nevertheless revive the inquiry as to the direction and fate of the expedition which "sailed in ten ships, under the direction of Prince Madoc, from North Wales, in the early part of the fourteenth century," and which it has been pretty clearly shown, I believe, landed somewhere on the coast of Florida or about the mouth of the Mississippi, and, according to the history and poetry of their own country, "settled somewhere in the interior of America, where they are yet remaining, intermixed with some of the Indian tribes."

I have not met in any other tribe anything in personal appearance or customs that would seem to account for the direction of this colony, but in several of the customs of this tribe which I have already described, as well as in others which I shall name, there appeared to exist striking proofs of the arrival and settlement of that colony in the western regions of America.

The Mandan mode of constructing their wigwams, already described, was almost precisely that of the rude mode of building their cabins amongst the peasantry of the mountains of Wales, and, as I am told, in some districts they are building them at the present day.

The *pottery* made by the Mandans, to the time of their destruction, was strikingly similar to that manufactured in parts of Wales at the present time, and exactly similar to that found in the tumuli on the banks of the Ohio and Muskingum rivers; strongly suggesting the probable fact that those people formerly inhabited the banks of those rivers, and by a great number of moves up the Missouri had arrived at the place where I found them.[32]

A peculiar and very beautiful sort of *blue beads* were also manufactured by the Mandans, and of which they were certainly the only known manufacturers in America; and since publishing my large work on the North American Indians, in which I gave some account of this curious manufacture, I have received several letters from Welsh gentlemen of science, one of whom enclosed me drawings from, and another the *beads themselves,* found in *tumuli,* and also in the present progress of manufacture in Wales, precisely the same in character, in shape, and in colour and composition, as those in my collection brought from the Mandans.

The manufacture of these blue beads by the Mandans was guarded as a profound secret until the time of their destruction, although the Fur Company had made them repeated and liberal offers if they would divulge it, as the Mandan beads commanded a much higher price amongst the Mandans and the neighbouring tribes to whom they bartered them, than the beads introduced by the fur traders.[33]

The *canoes* or boats of the Mandans, differing from those of all other tribes in America, were precisely the *Welsh coracle,* made of a bull's hide stretched over a frame of willow rods, bent and inter-locked, and *pulled* over the water by the paddle, in the same manner as the coracle is pulled, by reaching forward with the paddle instead of passing it by the side of the boat, which is nearly round, and the paddler seated or kneeling in its front.[34]

From the translation of their name, already mentioned, *Nu-mah-ká-kee* (pheasants), an important inference may be drawn in support of the probability of their having formerly lived much farther to the south, as that bird does not exist on the prairies of the Upper Missouri, and is not to be met with short of the heavy forests of Ohio and Indiana, one thousand eight hundred miles south of the last residence of the Mandans.

And in their familiar name of *Mandan,* which is not an Indian word, there are equally singular and important features. In the first place, that they knew nothing of the name or how they got it; and next, that the word *Mandan* in the Welsh language (it being purely a Welsh word) means *red dye,* of which further mention will be made.

In the brief vocabulary of Mandan words which I published in the Appendix to my large work on the North American Indians, it has been discovered by several Welsh scholars that there exist the following most striking resemblances, which it would be difficult to account for in any other way than that which I am now attempting.

ENGLISH.	MANDAN.	WELSH.
I	me	me
you	ne	chwe
he	e	a
she	ea	ea
it	ount	hwynt
we	noo	ne
they	eonah	hwna (*masculine*) hona (*feminine*)
no	negosh	nagosh
head	pan	pen
The Great Spirit	*Maho-Peneta*	*Mawr-Penaethir*[35]

From the above evidences, and others which might be produced, I fully believe, what perhaps will for ever remain impossible (positively) to prove, that the ten ships commanded by the brother of Prince Madoc, or some portion of them, entered the mouth of the Mississippi, and advanced up that noble river to the mouth of the Ohio, which could easily have been navigated by vessels of that date, and, advancing up that river, which they would naturally have chosen, as the broadest and most gentle stream, as far as their vessels could go, the adventurers planted themselves as agriculturists on its rich and fertile banks, where they lived and flourished and increased in numbers, until they were attacked, and at last besieged, by the numerous hordes of savages who were jealous of their growing condition; and as a protection against the Indian assaults built those civilized fortifications, the remains of which are so numerous on the banks of the Ohio and Muskingum Rivers.

In these defences, I believe, they were at length all destroyed by the overpowering numbers of the savage hordes, excepting those few families who had intermarried with the Indians, and whose offsprings, being *half-castes,* were in such a manner allied to them that their lives were spared.

Those, as is generally the case with the *half-castes,* I believe had formed a separate village in the vicinity of the whites, supporting themselves by their embroidery with porcupine quills, to which they gave the beautiful dyes for which the Mandans have been peculiarly famous, and were called by their Welsh neighbours, and in the Welsh language, the *Mandans* (or red dyers).

These *half-castes,* having formed themselves into a separate community, probably took up their residence, after the destruction of the whites, on the banks of the Missouri, on which, for the want of a permanent location and right to the soil, being on the lands and the hunting-grounds of their more powerful enemies, they were obliged repeatedly to move, as the numerous marks of their ancient residences show; and continuing their moves up the river, in time migrated to the place where I saw them, and where they terminated their existence.

Thus much of and for the character and modes of a peculiar people, who were proverbially intelligent, hospitable, and kind; who, with their language, have suddenly ceased to exist; whose character, history, modes, and personal appearance, almost solely existing in my collections, I have considered essentially interesting and important to *Ethnology,* and some of the most remarkable of which (as I have said) I am here, from a sense of *duty,* emphatically recording for the information of those who are to study *Man* and his modes after I shall be gone.[36]

GEO. CATLIN.

EST. PERPET.

The object of this detached page, which is proposed to be used at the discretion of the purchaser, is to complete the links in the chain of events in the singular custom which is described in the foregoing pages, as far as could properly be done for general reading.

Scientific men, who study, as has been said in the Preface, not the *proprieties* of man, but MAN, will receive this addendum in this form, and, I believe, duly appreciate and protect it.

The bizarre and frightful character already described as *O-ke-hée-de* (the owl or evil spirit) who approached the village from the prairies, and entered the area of the buffalo-dancers to the terror of the women and children, had attached, by a small thong encircling his waist, a buffalo's tail, behind; and from under a bunch of buffalo hair covering the pelvis, an artificial penis, ingeniously (and naturally) carved in wood, of colossal dimensions, pendulous as he ran, and extending somewhat below his knees. This was, like his body, painted jet-black, with the exception of the glans, which was of as glaring a red as vermilion could make it.

On entering the crowd where the buffalo-dance was being performed, he directed his steps towards the groups of women, who retreated in the greatest alarm, tumbling over each other, and screaming for help as he was advancing upon them, as well they might, from the change of aspect at that moment; for at his near approach to them he elevated with both hands his delicate wand, and as he raised it over their heads there was a corresponding rising of the penis, probably caused by some small, invisible thong connecting the two together.

The *medicine* pipe of the master of ceremonies being thrust before his eyes, its charm held him motionless for some minutes, until the women and children had retreated to a safe distance, when the pipe was gradually withdrawn, his wand lowered to the ground, and he regained his power of locomotion.

After several repeated attempts of this kind, and being defeated in the same way in each, he returned to the buffalo-dance, still continued, and being jostled (apparently by accident) against one of the eight buffalo-dancers, he stepped back, and looking at the animal, placed himself for a moment in the attitude of a buffalo bull in the rutting season; and mounting on to one of the dancing buffaloes, elevated his wand, and consequently the penis, which was inserted under the skin of the animal, whilst the man underneath continued to dance, with his body in a horizontal position.

An indescribable excitement was produced by the new position of this strange being, endeavouring to time his steps in the dance in which he was now (apparently) taking a part, with the motions of the animal under him. The women and children of the whole tribe, who were lookers-on, were instructed to clap their hands and shout their approbation, as they all wanted buffaloes to supply them with food during the coming year, and which supply they attributed to this indispensable form.

The usual time of the buffalo's leap was occupied in this singular affair, when this strange actor was down; and imitating perfectly the motions and noise of the buffalo bulls on such occasions, he approached and leaped four of the eight in succession, without in the least checking the dance, producing something like a quarter of an hour of the highest excitement and amusement of the crowd.

This scene finished (the buffaloes still dancing), *O-ke-hée-de* appeared much fatigued and exhausted, which brought the women and children around him, they being no longer afraid of him. The women danced up to him and back, in lascivious attitudes, tempting him with challenges which, with all his gallantry, he was now (apparently) unable to accept. It was in this distressing dilemma that his wand was broken, as has been described, and he was driven into the prairie, where he was again beset by a throng of women and children, and the frightful appendage was wrested from his body, and brought by its captor triumphantly into the village, wrapped in a bunch of wild sage, and carried in her arms as she would have carried an infant. She was escorted by two matrons on each side, who lifted her on to the front of the Medicine Lodge, directly over its door, from whence she harangued the multitude for some time, claiming that she held the power of creation, and of life and death over them; that she was the father of all the buffaloes, and that she could make them come or stay away as she pleased.

She then ordered the buffalo-dance to be stopped, and the *"Pohk-hong"* (or torturing scenes) to commence in the Medicine Lodge, as has been described. She demanded the handsomest dress in the Mandan tribe, which the master of ceremonies had in readiness, and presented to her, as he received from her hands the singular trophy, and which he deposited, no doubt, amongst the sacred archives of the nation, and appointed her to the envied position of conductress of the *Feast of the Buffaloes*, to be given that night, as has been described.

GEO. CATLIN.

APPENDIX

No. I.—CERTIFICATE.

"We hereby certify that we witnessed, in company with Mr. Catlin, in the Mandan village, the ceremony represented in the four paintings to which this certificate refers, and that he has therein represented those scenes as we saw them transacted, without any addition or exaggeration.

> J. KIPP, *Agent of the American Fur Company.*
> J. CRAWFORD, *Clerk.*
> ABRAHAM BOGARD.

Mandan Village, 28th July, 1832."

Witnessing scenes so extraordinary as those described in the foregoing pages, and so remote from civilization, I deemed it prudent to obtain the above certificates, which were given in the Mandan village, and inseparably attached to the backs of my four original oil-paintings of those four days' ceremonies, made in the Mandan village, and submitted to the examination and approval of the chiefs and the whole tribe, and now in my possession, entirely unchanged.

No. II.

"Fort Gibson, Arkansaw, June 3rd, 1836.
To GEORGE CATLIN, Esq.

Dear Sir,

I have seen your account of the religious ceremonies of the Mandans, and no man will give you so much credit for it as myself. I conducted the American Fur Company's business with the Mandans for eight years before Mr. Kipp, and was the first white man who ever learned to speak the Mandan language.

Mr. Kipp, Mr. Crawford, and Bogard, who have given you their certificates, are old acquaintances of mine, and I am glad you had them with you. All those parts of the ceremonies which you describe as taking place outside of the Medicine Lodge,— the *bull dance*, the *dragging scene*, etc., I witnessed annually for eight years just as you have represented them, and I was every year an invited guest to the *"feast of the buffaloes,"* but I was always unable to get admission into the Medicine Lodge to see that part of the tortures that took place inside.

TILTON,
Sutler to the First Regiment of Mounted Dragoons."

No. III.—DESTRUCTION OF THE MANDANS.

As to the unlucky fate of the Mandans, the following letter, enclosed to me by my esteemed friend Thomas Potts, Esq., of Edinburgh, and now in my possession, written by his brother, who was then a clerk in the Fur Company's employment, is worthy of being read and distinctly understood, and will be received as undeniable authority, as he could have no *motive* for misrepresentation.

"Mandan Village, Upper Missouri, October 1, 1837.
To THOMAS POTTS, Esq., Edinburgh, Scotland.

Dear Brother,

. . . The friendly and hospitable tribe of Mandans are nearly all destroyed by the smallpox. There are but thirty-two families remaining, and those chiefly women and children; these the Riccarrees, who have moved up and taken possession, have turned out of the village, after plundering them of everything they had on earth, and they will all be destroyed by their enemies the Sioux, as they have no weapons to defend themselves with.

About sixty young warriors, who had recovered from the smallpox, on seeing how they were disfigured, put an end to their existence by stabbing or drowning themselves. Nothing now but the name of these people remains.

The disease was brought up by the Fur Company's steamboat in the spring: two men on board were sick with the disease when the boat arrived at the Mandan village, and the Mandans who went on board caught the infection, hence the almost total destruction of the tribe.

The Indians are much exasperated against the whites; indeed, if they were not very forbearing, they would destroy every white man in the country, as they have been the cause of all the distress and disease, which have gone also to all the neighbouring tribes, and may perhaps depopulate the whole country. . . .

Your affectionate Brother,
ANDREW POTTS."

No. IV.—DESTRUCTION OF THE MANDANS.

In the summer following the calamity of the Mandans, Mr. Kennith M'Kenzie, at that time chief factor of the Fur Company, and in charge of Fort Union, at the mouth of the Yellow Stone River, came down to St. Louis and New York, where I had an interview with him; and as he was taking leave, to return to the Yellow Stone, passing through the Mandan village, I placed in his hands the sum of fifty dollars, and begged him to procure and send to me any relics of the Mandans that he might think interesting to be preserved in my Indian Collection.

In the course of the ensuing summer I received the following letter, enclosed in a box containing some articles procured for me, as described within it. Mr. M'Kenzie, who was from the city of Edinburgh, had treated me with honour and much kindness when I was visiting the Mandans and other tribes on the Upper Missouri a few years previous, and I never believed that he had any motive for misrepresentation in the following letter:—

"Fort Mandan, Mandan Village, Upper Missouri,
June, 1839.
To George Catlin, Esq., City of New York.

Dear Sir,

. . . I have sent this day by our boat a box containing a few articles of Mandan manufacture, such as I thought would be of interest to you for your Collection; but as the Riccarrees have taken possession of the Mandan village they have appropriated nearly everything, and it is impossible therefore to obtain what I otherwise would have procured for you. I have sent you, however, one thing which you will peculiarly value,—the famous *war-knife* of your old friend *Mah-to-toh-pa*, the war chief. This knife and its history you are familiar with.

I have also sent a very beautiful woman's robe, with a figure of the sun painted on it, a grizzly bear's-claw necklace, and several other articles, the best I could obtain. . . . On reaching here I learn that amongst the Assiniboins and Crees about 7000, and amongst the Blackfeet 15,000, have fallen victims to the disease, which spread to those tribes.

Of the Mandans between forty and fifty were all that were left when the disease subsided. The Riccarrees soon after moved up and took possession of their village, making slaves of the remaining Mandans, and are living in it at the present time.

A few months after the Riccarrees took possession they were attacked by a war-party of Sioux, and in the middle of the battle the Mandans, men, women, and children, whilst fighting for the Riccarrees, at a concerted signal ran through the pickets and threw themselves under the horses' feet of the Sioux, and, still fighting, begged the

Sioux to kill them 'that they might not live to be the dogs of the Riccarrees.' The last of the tribe were here slain.

Yours truly,

KENNITH M'KENZIE."

I might not have encumbered my work with the above certificates and extracts of letters in my possession, were it not that the very Company who have been the cause of the destruction of these people, to punish me for having condemned their system of rum and whisky selling, and to veil their iniquities, have endeavoured to throw discredit upon my descriptions of the religious ceremonies of the Mandans, and to induce the world to believe, contrary to my representations, that a large proportion of the Mandans still exist, and are rapidly increasing under the *nourishing auspices of the Fur Company*.

There is no doubt whatever that a few straggling Mandans who fled to the Minatarrees, or in other directions, are still existing, nor any doubt but that the Riccarrees, since the destruction of the Mandans, have occupied to this day the Mandan village, under the range of the guns of the Fur Company's fort, and are exhibited to the passers-by and represented to the reading world as *surviving Mandans*. The policy of this is easily understood, and the reader who has paid attention to the foregoing certificates and extracts of letters, added to my own testimony as an eye-witness, will have no difficulty in drawing correct conclusions as to the peculiar customs and the cruel fate of the Mandan Indians.

Every reader of this work will have a knowledge of, and a respect for the names of Cass and Webster, who were familiar with my works and also with Indian history and Indian character.

Letter from GENERAL CASS, *American Ambassador to France, and since, Secretary of State of the United States of America.*

"Légation des États-Unis à Paris.

Dear Sir,

No man can appreciate better than myself the admirable fidelity of your Indian Collection and Indian book, which I have lately examined. They are equally spirited and accurate; they are true to nature. Things that *are,* are not sacrificed, as they too often are by the painter, to things as (in his judgment) they should be.

During eighteen years of my life I was superintendant of Indian affairs in the North-west Territory of the United States, and during more than five I was Secretary of War, to which department belongs the general control of Indian concerns. I know the Indians thoroughly. I have spent many a month in their camps, council-houses, villages, and hunting-grounds; I have fought *with* them and *against* them; and I have negotiated seventeen treaties of peace or of cession with them. I mention these circumstances to show you that I have a good right to speak confidently upon the subject of your drawings. Among them I recognize many of my old acquaintances, and everywhere I am struck with the vivid representations of them and their customs, of their peculiar features, and of their costumes. Unfortunately, they are receding before the advancing tide of our population, and are probably destined at no distant day wholly to disappear; but your Collection will preserve them, as far as human art can do, and will form the most perfect monument of an extinguished race that the world has ever seen.

To GEORGE CATLIN.

LEWIS CASS."

Extract from the Speech of the Hon. DANIEL WEBSTER, *on a Motion in the Senate of the United States, for the purchase of Catlin's Indian Collection in* 1849.

"Mr. President,—The question is, whether it does not become us, as a useful thing, to possess in the United States this collection of paintings, etc., made amongst the Indian tribes?—whether it is not a case for the exercise of *large liberality,* I will not say *bounty,* but *policy?* These tribes, Sir, that have preceded us, to whose lands we have succeeded, and who have no written memorials of their laws, their habits, and their manners, are all passing away to the land of forgetfulness. Their likeness, manners, and customs, are portrayed with more accuracy and truth in this Collection by Catlin than in all the other drawings and representations on the face of the earth. Somebody in this country ought to possess this Collection,—that is my opinion; and I do not know who there is, or where there is to be found, any society or individual, who or which can with so much propriety possess himself or itself of it as the Government of the United States. For my part, then, I do think that the preservation of Catlin's Indian Collection in this country is an *important public act.* I think it properly belongs to those accumulations of historical matters respecting our predecessors on this continent which it is very proper for the Government of the United States to maintain. As I have said, this race is going into forgetfulness; they track the continuation of mankind in the present age, and call recollection back to them. And here they are better exhibited, in my judgment, better set forth and presented to the mind, and the taste and the curiosity of mankind, than in all other collections in the world. I go for this as an *American* subject, as a thing belonging to us, to our history, to the history of a race whose lands we till, and over whose obscure graves and bones we tread every day. I look upon it as a thing more appropriate for us than the ascertaining of the South Pole, or anything that can be discovered in the Dead Sea or the river Jordan. These are the grounds, Sir, upon which I propose to proceed, and I shall vote for the appropriation with great pleasure."[37]

THE END.

ON THE ACCURACY OF CATLIN'S ACCOUNT OF THE MANDAN CEREMONIES.*

BY JAMES KIPP.

We publish the following letter as an act of justice to the memory of the late Mr. Catlin, and as a verification of the truth of his account of a very interesting ceremony among the Mandan Indians, a tribe now extinct. The ceremony was especially interesting in its resemblance to some of the self-inflicted tortures of the devotees of eastern superstitions. In regard to the remarks relative to Mr. Schoolcraft, it is but justice to state that we were intimately acquainted with him, and cannot for a moment harbor the thought that he would have done anything to disparage the veracity of any one from any other motive than a desire to promote the truth. The statements of Mr. Catlin were at the time so remarkable, the ceremonies which he described being so unlike those of other Indian tribes, that Mr. Schoolcraft was justifiable in receiving the account with doubt, although he may have expressed his disbelief in stronger terms than he would have done had he been more intimately acquainted with the character of Mr. Catlin than he appears to have been.—[J. H.]

"BARRY, *Clay County, Mo., August* 12, 1872.

DEAR SIR: Though a stranger to you, I take the liberty of addressing you this note as important to science and to the ethnology of our country, as well as important to the reputation of one who has devoted much of a long and hazardous life in portraying and perpetuating the customs of the dying races of man in America. Mr. Schoolcraft sent me, some years past, a copy of a large work he had published for the Government of the United States on the North American Indians, and of which work some thousands of copies were presented by the Government to the libraries of the institutions of the New and the Old World. In this work I find that Mr. Schoolcraft denies the truth of Mr. Catlin's description of the Mandan religious ceremonies—the truth of his assertion that the Mandan youths suspended the weight of their

*Smithsonian Institution, *Annual Report for 1872,* pp. 436–38.

bodies by splints run through the flesh on the breast and shoulders, &c.; and asserts, also, that his whole account of the Mandan religion is all wrong. It is a great pity that Mr. Schoolcraft, who never visited the Mandans, should have put forth such false and unfounded assertions as these on a subject so important to science, and so well established by proved facts.

I had the sole control of the American Fur Company's business with the Mandans, and lived in their village, for the space of thirteen years, from 1822 to 1835, and was doubtless the first white man who ever learned to speak their language. In the summer of 1832 Mr. George Catlin was a guest in my fort at the Mandan village, observing and learning the customs of those interesting and peculiar people, and painting the portraits of their celebrated men, of which he made many and with great exactness. It was during that summer that Mr. Catlin witnessed the Mandan religious ceremonies, the O-kee-pa described in his notes of travels among the North American Indians, and to which Mr. Schoolcraft has applied the insulting epithet of falsity in his great work. By the certificate published by Mr. Catlin, signed by my chief clerk and myself, on the 28th day of July, 1832, in the Mandan village, certifying that we witnessed, in company with Mr. Catlin, the whole of those four days' ceremonies, and that he has represented in his four paintings, then and there made of them, exactly what we saw, and without addition or exaggeration, it will be seen that I witnessed those scenes with Mr. Catlin and interpreted their whole meaning for him as they are described in his work. Since the extinction of this friendly tribe, and the end of this peculiar and unaccountable custom, and in the eighty-fifth year of my own age, from a sense of duty to my ancient friend Mr. Catlin, and a wish for the truthfulness of history, I have taken the liberty of committing to your care and for your use, as you may be disposed, the foregoing statements.

Yours, truly,

Professor HENRY,
   Smithsonian Institution.   JAMES KIPP."

EDITOR'S NOTES TO *O-KEE-PA*

1. George Catlin presumably cited *Life Amongst the Indians* because it was his most recent work. Subtitled *A Book for Youth,* it was a lively and popular first-person account of his travels among the Indians of North and South America, first published in London in 1861. It was reprinted in Paris (1863), and in London and New York (1867).

2. Speculation on the origin and antiquity of the American Indians was rife among scholars in Catlin's time. Catlin's theories on this score doubtless were influenced by the beliefs of his friend, Baron von Humboldt. For a concise statement on this subject by a leading modern student of Plains Indian prehistory see Waldo R. Wedel, *Prehistoric Man on the Great Plains,* Chap. 3, "The Early Big Game Hunters," pp. 46–78.

3. Catlin has reference to his brief view of the Mandans while the steamboat *Yellowstone* stopped at Fort Clark on its ascent of the Missouri in June 1832, as well as his longer sojourn at Fort Clark on his downriver journey in late July and early August of that summer. In all, his firsthand observation of the Mandans did not exceed three weeks to a month. He never saw them again after 1832.

4. Catlin was not aware of the visits to the Mandans by the traders Jacques D'Eglise (1790), John Evans (1796), David Thompson (1797), and Alexander Henry (1806), cited in the introduction to this volume. Accounts of their travels were not published until after Catlin's death in 1872.

5. After a review of the available information, including the published observations of Catlin and the early fur traders, the physical anthropologist Marshall T. Newman concluded that "the blondism and other non-Indian characteristics reported for the Mandans of the 18th and early 19th centuries are much more plausibly explained by intertribal and individual variability in pigmentation and facial features, augmented by recent White admixture, than by pre-Columbian miscegenation with European exploring parties." See Marshall T. Newman, "The Blond Mandan: A Critical Review of an Old Problem."

6. This hairdress was not peculiar to the Mandans. Catlin himself observed it among the Crows who visited Fort Union in the summer of 1832, whose men were renowned for their long hair, and whose chief "Long-hair" was reputed to have the longest locks of any Indian of the Upper Missouri, estimated by Catlin to have measured 10 feet 7 inches long. Catlin, *Letters and Notes on the Manners, Customs and Condition of the North American Indians, 1,* 49–50.

7. Although Prince Maximilian, in his *Travels in the Interior of North America,* p. 372, stated that it was celebrated "in the spring or summer," and, since he was not among the Mandans during those seasons, he was able to describe the ceremony only from the testimony of informants whom he consulted during the fall and winter of 1833–34. Bowers' elderly Mandan informants of 1930–31 told him that the O-kee-pa was performed when the willows were in full leaf, and before the summer tribal buffalo hunt. See Alfred W. Bowers, *Mandan Social and Ceremonial Organization,* p. 122.

8. Catlin's oil painting of this scene, entitled *A Bird's-Eye View of the Mandan Village, 1,800 Miles Above St. Louis,* is Cat. No. 386,474 in the Catlin Collection of the Smithsonian Institution.

9. Bowers (1950, p. 113) explained that this wall of cottonwood planks surrounded a red-painted cedar. The cedar was a symbol of the body of Lone Man (who in Mandan mythology was the instructor and protector of the tribe), and the planks were a symbol of the wall he had erected to protect the people from the flood.

10. Maximilian (1843, p. 372) referred to the O-kee-pa simply as "the penitential ceremony of the ark." Although Bowers' (1950, p. 339) aged, twentieth-century informants did not agree about the major reasons for performing the O-kee-pa, bringing buffalo to the village, informing young people of their tribal history, and enabling young men to fast were all mentioned as important justifications for this ceremony.

11. Lone Man, who opened the O-kee-pa ceremony, was the most important Mandan deity, and his role was always played by a prominent tribal leader (Bowers, pp. 118–20).

12. Catlin may possibly have confused this collection of edged tools or instruments of iron or steel with the collection of knives for cutting the flesh of the men who were to undergo the self-torture in the medicine lodge (see Bowers, p. 125). Maximilian (p. 373) was told that "all kinds of valuable articles, such as guns, robes, blankets, &c., are thrown towards him (Lone Man), of which he afterwards takes possession, while on his part he distributes pemmican among the people."

13. Evidently the number of young men who presented themselves for the torture varied greatly from year to year, as Maximilian stated. The German scientist also

was given to understand that the young men submitted "their bodies to a penance or certain tortures, in order to render themselves acceptable to the lord of life and the first man." (Maximilian, p. 373.)

14. The conductor of the O-kee-pa was a tribal leader or a rising man of great courage whose prominent role in this ceremony would prepare him for leadership in the eyes of his fellows. Maximilian (p. 373) observed that Mato-topé (Four Bears) had been selected to direct the ceremony in 1834. He was second chief of the tribe, an outstanding warrior, whom Catlin termed, the "most popular man in the nation" (Catlin, 1841, *1*, 145). Catlin painted his portrait twice, once in his picturesque dress costume, and once bare to the waist, showing the scars received when he had experienced the self-torture in the O-kee-pa some years earlier. Catlin's oils of both portraits are in the Smithsonian Institution (Cat. Nos. 386,128 and 386,131).

15. This was Mah-to-he-hah, Old Bear, whose portrait Catlin painted at full-length carrying his sacred medicine pipes, one in each hand. Catlin's oil portrait of this subject (Cat. No. 386,129 in the Smithsonian collection) is reproduced as Plate 55 in Catlin, 1841, Vol. 1.

16. This certificate is reprinted, with Catlin's comment, in the appendix to this volume, p. 87. Catlin also was accustomed to obtain signed statements from prominent traders or government officials who were present when he painted some of his most remarkable Indian portraits as testimony to the fact that the Indians had posed for him in the costumes portrayed and that the facial likenesses were faithful.

17. Bowers (pp. 112, 134) reproduced a drawing of the O-kee-pa ceremonial lodge executed from memory for him by the aged Mandan White Calf, and a plan of the interior of the lodge prior to the torture feature, which he designated "After Catlin."

18. Maynadier (see p. 27 of this volume) observed these turtle drums in the ceremony of 1860, and stated his belief that they were stuffed with hair rather than filled with water. Bowers (p. 151 and Fig. 18) saw and pictured one of these drums which was still owned by an aged Mandan in 1930. It was of buffalo hide, stretched over an oak frame. Small balls of buffalo hair were placed inside the drums to symbolize the spirits of unborn buffalo.

19. Bowers (pp. 111, 131–32) found that the name O-kee-pa (or Okipa) for this ceremony meant "to look alike," and that it was derived from the Mandan concept that the bull dancers should be of the same size and be painted and dressed alike. Bowers and Maximilian (1843, p. 374) agreed with Catlin that they were eight in number, and Catlin appears to have been especially keen in his observation of the painting of an infant on the abdomen of each bull dancer. However, both Maximilian and Bowers assert that the bull dancer's costume had but one horn, rather than the

two Catlin pictures in Plate VI. Maynadier, our only eyewitness recorder of this ceremony besides Catlin, seemed to have been more interested in the actions of the bull dancers than in a minute description of their striking costumes. (See pp. 27–30 this volume.)

20. Maximilian (p. 376) mentioned the two dancers painted black with white stars to represent night; but he failed to list the two symbolizing day. However, Bowers (pp. 131–32) was told there were two of each of these dancers.

21. Maximilian (pp. 374–76) mentioned all of these birds and animals impersonated by appropriately painted and costumed dancers who mimicked the actions of the creatures they represented. He agreed that there were two of each, except for the antelopes, comprising "forty or fifty Indians of different ages."

22. Bowers (pp. 131–32) was told of thirty-four characters participating in the ceremonies during the third day, in addition to the antelopes whose numbers varied from year to year and were composed of unselected volunteers.

23. Catlin's more frank and detailed description of the appearance and actions of the Evil Spirit (or Foolish One) will be found in his *Folium Reservatum* on pp. 83–85 of this volume. Although Maximilian (pp. 375–76) gives a more restrained description of this primitive clown's antics, Bowers' account (pp. 144–46) of the part played by this character indicates that Catlin's explanation of his actions is *not* an exaggeration.

24. The sacrifice of fingers or portions of fingers by those who participated in the O-kee-pa was also reported by Maximilian (p. 377). However, self-mutilation, in mourning for the loss of dear relatives, was common among the tribes of the northern Great Plains and was reported by a number of field observers. Lewis and Clark were visited by the son of a Mandan chief who had but recently died on October 24, 1804, and Clark recorded that "this man has his two little fingers off, on inquiring the cause, was told it was customary for this nation to Show their greaf by some testimony of pain, and that it was not uncommon for them to take off 2 Smaller fingers of the hand (at the 2d joints) and some times more with other marks of Savage affection." *Original Journals of the Lewis and Clark Expedition,* ed. Reuben Gold Thwaites, *1, 205.*

25. Maximilian (p. 377) also wrote a vivid description of this "last race" (although he did not use that term). "Two men, who have no part in the festival, take one of the penitents between them, hold him by the hand, and the whole circle moves round with the greatest rapidity. . . . The famished and tortured penitents, for the most part, soon fall down, and many faint away, but no regard is paid to this; they are dragged and pulled about as long as they can possibly bear it; they are then let loose, and remain stretched on the ground as if dead."

26. Lt. Maynadier's description of the self-torture, which he witnessed in the Mandan O-kee-pa of 1860, is a very graphic one, and corroborates Catlin's observations (see pp. 28–29 of this volume). Self-torture, through the insertion of wooden skewers into the breasts, and the attachment of rawhide lines to an upright center post, from which the suppliant was required to tear himself loose—painfully and under severe nervous shock—was practiced in the sun dances of more than a dozen Plains Indian tribes. It was reported as early as 1805 among the Arikara and Hidatsa (neighbors of the Mandans) and persisted until 1891 among the Blood Indians of Alberta. R. N. Wilson photographed that last performance. (See John C. Ewers, "Self-torture in the Blood Indian Sun Dance," pp. 166–73 and Fig. 2.)

27. Bowers (p. 150) was informed that the knives and edged tools were thrown into the Missouri River as an offering to the Grandfather Snake.

28. Alexander Henry may have witnessed this sequel to a performance of the O-kee-pa in a Mandan village as early as July 19, 1806 (see pp. 9–10 this volume). However, he made no reference to the O-kee-pa. Actually it appears to have been even more closely associated with the winter buffalo calling rites of the Mandans, described by Lewis and Clark on pp. 6–7 of this volume, and recently, under the name of the Red Stick Ceremony, by Bowers (pp. 315–19). Bowers interviewed aged Mandan women who had "walked with the buffalo," as they called this rite. They believed that this act of adultery under ceremonial conditions actually strengthened their marriage bonds, and that they had served as means of transmitting to their husbands power which would bring them success in hunting and warfare (Bowers, p. 336).

29. Mandan myths regarding the origin of the O-kee-pa were many and varied, and Catlin recorded only a portion of one of them (see Bowers, pp. 156–63, 347–61).

30. The sacred number four occurred in ceremonial contexts among a number of Plains Indian tribes. Among the Blackfeet, an Algonquian-speaking tribe unrelated to the Mandans, Clark Wissler found: "When something has been dreamed four times it becomes at once a medicine of certain power. Again, a man seldom refuses the fourth request for a thing: but should he, the petitioner feels insulted." *Ceremonial Bundles of the Blackfoot Indians,* p. 247.

31. Catlin was misinformed regarding the extinction of the Mandans in the smallpox epidemic of 1837. Although estimates of the numbers of survivors vary, Hayden's figure of 23 men, 40 women, and 60 to 70 young persons may be nearly correct. He also reckoned the Mandans at "about 35 or 40 huts, nearly 300 persons" in 1855 (Hayden, *Contributions to the Ethnography and Philology of the Indian Tribes of the Upper Missouri,* pp. 433–34). The official census of 1890, at the time of the last O-kee-pa performance, listed 251 Mandans on the Fort Berthold Reservation.

32. Archaeologists have found pottery in sites of the Missouri Valley in the Dakotas which date back to before 500 or 800 of this era. In historic times the Hidatsa and Arikara as well as the Mandan of this region were skilled potters (Wedel, *Prehistoric Man in the Great Plains,* pp. 165, 205).

33. Pierre-Antoine Tabeau, a fur trader among the Arikaras at the time of Lewis and Clark, stated that people of that tribe had been taught the art of melting and molding glass trade beads by a Spanish prisoner (presumably late in the eighteenth century). The available evidence would suggest that the Mandans learned this art from the Arikaras. See Stirling, "Arikara Glassworking."

34. The bull boat, of willow framework covered with buffalo hide, was used by the Mandans, Hidatsas, and Arikaras for crossing the Missouri and for short trips on the river. Since it was fashioned of perishable materials, evidences of the bull boat have not been found archaeologically in this region.

35. Probably Catlin was not aware of John Evans' failure to find Welsh-speaking Indians on the Upper Missouri in 1796 (see pp. 4–5 of this volume). Amateur linguists, by comparative lists of a few selected words, have proposed a number of relationships between New and Old World languages. But professional linguists, who compare structures of languages as well, regard Mandan as a dialect of the Siouan family of languages. Other Siouan dialects were spoken by Indian tribes as widely separated as the Crows of Montana, Biloxi of Mississippi, Winnebago of Wisconsin, and Catawba of South Carolina during the historic period. See "Siouan Family" in Hodge, ed., *Handbook of American Indians North of Mexico,* pp. 577–79.

36. Catlin does not state how he learned of the Welsh Indian theory, but it was current as early as 1730 when Rev. Morgan Jones claimed that his life was spared by the Tuscarora Indians because he prayed in the Welsh language, which was the same as their own. Others have attempted to identify Madoc's mythical explorers with the Nottoway, Croatan, Modoc, Hopi, Comanche, Pawnee, Kansa, and Oto tribes. See "Welsh Indians" in Hodge, ed., *Handbook of American Indians North of Mexico,* pp. 931–32. A more recent effort has been made to prove that the Mandans and their culture were influenced by fourteenth-century Scandinavian explorers. However, H. R. Holand's theories, expressed in *Westward from Vinland* (1940), are no less romantic than Catlin's attempt to prove an early Welsh influence upon the Mandans.

37. Despite Daniel Webster's eloquent plea, the bill for the purchase of Catlin's Indian Gallery by the United States failed to pass the Senate by the margin of a single vote. George Catlin had been dead for six years when Mrs. Joseph Harrison presented the great majority of the paintings and artifacts to the nation on May 19, 1879. They are now preserved in the Smithsonian Institution.

EDITOR'S BIBLIOGRAPHY

ARCHIVAL MATERIALS

NEW YORK PUBLIC LIBRARY, RARE BOOK ROOM: George Catlin's letter to Prince Maximilian of Wied-Neuwied, Dec. 2, 1866.

SMITHSONIAN INSTITUTION ARCHIVES: Joseph Henry's Diary (for the year 1872); Joseph Henry's Correspondence, Letters sent, 1866–72.

YALE UNIVERSITY LIBRARY, WESTERN AMERICANA COLLECTION: *An Account of an Annual Religious Ceremony Practised by the Mandan Tribe of North American Indians* (unauthorized printing, 1865); George Catlin's manuscript, "O-KEE-PA, a RELIGIOUS CEREMONY (and other customs) of the MANDANS," and proofs thereof dated Feb. 12 and May 17 (1867); proof and revised proof of George Catlin's *Folium Reservatum*, dated May 11 and May 17 (1867).

NEWSPAPERS

New-York Commercial Advertiser: George Catlin's letters from the Upper Missouri, July 24, 1832; Oct. 20, 1832; Nov. 13, 1832; Jan. 10, 1833; Feb. 20, 1833.

BOOKS AND PERIODICALS

American Journal of Science and Arts, 35, 1838–39.

Boller, Henry A., *Among the Indians: Eight Years in the Far West, 1858–1866,* Philadelphia, 1868.

———, "The Letters of Henry A. Boller: Upper Missouri Fur Trader," ed. R. H. Mattison, *North Dakota History, 33* (1966), 108–219.

Bowers, Alfred W., *Mandan Social and Ceremonial Organization,* Chicago, 1950.

Bruner, Edward M., "Mandan," in *Perspectives in American Indian Culture Change*, ed. Edward H. Spicer, Chicago, 1961.

Catlin, George, *Catalogue of Catlin's Indian Gallery*, New York, 1837.

—— *Letters and Notes on the Manners, Customs and Condition of the North American Indians*, 2 vols., London, 1841.

—— *Life Amongst the Indians*, London, 1861.

—— *Lifted and Subsided Rocks of North America*, London, 1870.

—— *O-kee-pa: A Religious Ceremony and Other Customs of the Mandans*, London, 1867.

Chittenden, Hiram M., *The American Fur Trade of the Far West*, 2 vols., New York, 1902.

Ewers, John C., Self-torture in the Blood Indian Sun Dance, *Journal, Washington Academy of Sciences, 38* (1948), 166–73.

—— The Indian Trade of the Upper Missouri before Lewis and Clark: An Interpretation, *Bulletin, Missouri Historical Society*, St. Louis, *10* (1954), 429–40.

—— George Catlin, Painter of Indians and the West, *Annual Report, Smithsonian Institution* for 1955, Washington, D.C., 1956, pp. 483–528.

Gaskin, L.J.P., A Rare Pamphlet on the Mandan Religious Ceremony, in the Library of the Horniman Museum, *Man* (Sept. 1939), 141–42.

Hayden, Ferdinand V., Contributions to the Ethnography and Philology of the Indian Tribes of the Missouri Valley, *Transactions, American Philosophical Society, 12* (1862), 2.

Henry, Alexander, and David Thompson, *New Light on the Early History of the Greater Northwest*, ed. Elliott Coues, 3 vols., New York, 1897.

Hodge, Frederick Webb, ed., *Handbook of American Indians North of Mexico*, Bureau of American Ethnology, Bulletin 30, 2 vols., Washington, 1907–10.

Holand, H. R., *Westward from Vinland*, New York, 1940.

Jackson, Donald, ed., *Letters of the Lewis and Clark Expedition with Related Documents, 1783–1854*, Urbana, Ill., 1962.

Kipp, James, On the Accuracy of Catlin's Account of the Mandan Ceremonies, *Annual Report, Board of Regents Smithsonian Institution for 1872*, Washington, 1873, pp. 436–38.

La Verendrye, P. G. V., *Journals and Letters of Pierre Gaultier de Varennes de la Verendrye and his Sons*, ed. Lawrence J. Burpee, Champlain Society Publication 16, Toronto, 1927.

Lewis, Meriwether, and William Clark, *History of the Expedition under the Command of Lewis and Clark*, ed. Elliott Coues, 4 vols., New York, 1893.

—— *Original Journals of the Lewis and Clark Expedition*, ed. Reuben Gold Thwaites, 8 vols., New York, 1904–05.

Matthews, Washington, *Ethnography and Philology of the Hidatsa Indians*, U.S. Geological and Geographical Survey Miscellaneous Publication No. 7, Washington, 1877.

Maximilian Alexander Philip, Prince of Wied-Neuwied, *Travels in the Interior of North America*, London, 1843.

Morgan, Lewis Henry, *Lewis Henry Morgan: The Indian Journals, 1859–1862*, ed. Leslie A. White, Ann Arbor, 1959.

Nasatir, A. P., ed., *Before Lewis and Clark; Documents Illustrating the History of the Missouri, 1785–1804*, 2 vols., St. Louis, 1952.

Newman, Marshall T., The Blond Mandan: A Critical Review of an Old Problem, *Southwestern Journal of Anthropology, 6* (1950), 255–72.

Raynolds, W. F., *Report on the Exploration of the Yellowstone and the Country Drained by That River*, Senate Executive Document, 77, 40th Congress, 1st Session, Washington, 1868.

Roehm, Marjorie Catlin, ed., *The Letters of George Catlin and His Family*, Berkeley and Los Angeles, 1966.

Schoolcraft, Henry Rowe, *Historical and Statistical Information Respecting the History, Condition, and Prospects of the Indian Tribes of the United States*, 6 vols., Philadelphia, 1851–57.

Stirling, Matthew W., Arikara Glassworking, *Journal of the Washington Academy of Sciences, 37* (1947), 257–63.

Thompson, David, *David Thompson's Narrative of His Explorations in Western America, 1784–1812*, ed. J. B. Tyrrell, Champlain Society Publication No. 12, Toronto, 1916.

Wedel, Waldo R., *Prehistoric Man on the Great Plains*, Norman, Okla., 1961.

Will, G. F., and H. J. Spinden, The Mandans. A Study of Their Culture, Archaeology and Language, *Papers of the Peabody Museum of American Archaeology and Ethnology, Harvard University, 3*, No. 4 (1906).

Williams, David, John Evans' Strange Journey, *American Historical Review, 54*, Nos. 2, 3 (1949), 277–95, 508–29.

Wissler, Clark, *Ceremonial Bundles of the Blackfoot Indians*, American Museum of Natural History, Anthropological Papers, 7, No. 2 (1912).

Wood, W. Raymond, *An Interpretation of Mandan Culture History*, Bureau of American Ethnology, Bulletin 198, Washington, D.C. (in press).

INDEX